MY FAVORITE FAVORITE MEOW-WORKER IS

_____

Dedication

This book is dedicated to all the ones who have "furry" colleagues and coworkers at home!

You are my inspiration in producing books and I'm excited to help in the planning of some fun for all the "Meow–Workers" around the world!

How to Use this My Favorite Meow-Worker Notebook:

The purpose of my favorite meow-worker journal is to keep all your various work at home and keepsake memories of working with your pet at home organized in one easy to find spot.

Here are some simple guidelines to follow so you can make the most of using this book:

1. The first "My Favorite Meow-Worker" section is for you to write out what you want to say to your favorite pet at home… so you can go back there to be reminded of your journey at home…

2. Most ideas are inspired by something we have seen. Use the "The Things I Love" section to use the checklist of all the things your meow-worker loves…

3. The "Paw Print Blank Journal" section is for you to write out all the things you imagine your favorite pet doing and record your journey of spending time at home with your favorite pets…

4. And even more pages with the "Photo Frame" section is great for taking pics of your favorite co-worker doing "work" at home.

5. The "Favorite Place to Run" section is for you to keep a visual reminder of each place your favorite pet enjoys frantically running around.

6. The "Times you made me laugh so hard" section is for you to describe your at home entertainment and the funny things your pet has done.

7. The "Favorite Place To Nap" section is for you to write out the time of day and place that your meow-worker likes to go to have a daily cat nap. And any especially helpful information for remembering later on.

8. The "You were productive at "work" today is for you to write out keepsake memories of how you're feeling about working with your pet at home, your story, your journey so you can be reminded later on.

9. Whether you've just started working at home with your favorite pet, or it's been years now. You will want to write down all your enjoyment in this notebook to look back on and always remember the things you want to say to your favorite co-worker.

10. This My Favorite Meow-Worker Log Book makes a great gift for any cat-loving person that works at home with their best friend and favorite pet! Size is 8 X 10 inches, 112 pages, soft matte finish cover.

My Favorite Meow-Worker

Dear Meow-Worker, thanks for being my supportive four-legged "co-worker" at home today and I wanted to tell you that I love…

This is what it's like "working together" with you at home…

This is what I imagine you doing in the other room right now…

Today, you make me happy by…

Your favorite snack is… | Favorite place to sit is… | Your rating in the Snuggles department is… ☆☆☆☆☆

I am feeding you your favorite… | The times you made me laugh so hard are… | I love it when you…

I could use some more… | I could use a little less… | When you roll over, you…

On our "break time" from work, you love to… | | Fave place to frantically run…

When I wash you, you… | My "support system" includes… | I find it funny when…

Some lessons I learned from knowing you are… | | Favorite place to leave hairballs is…

Your favorite place to be scratched is…. | The sound you make is… | Your favorite place to nap is…

You licked me this many times… | We snuggled this many times… | Favorite TV show is…

You were productive at "work" today by… | Your favorite toy to play with is… | You love to torture the…

Things I love

- [ ] Toys
- [ ] Cat nip
- [ ] Getting snuggles
- [ ] Purring
- [ ] Playtime
- [ ] Headbutting
- [ ] Laser pointers
- [ ] Treats for being cute
- [ ] Rubbing against legs
- [ ] Meowing for attention
- [ ] Sitting on the keyboard
- [ ] Licking my owner's neck
- [ ] "Meetings" with my new manager at home
- [ ] Waking my owner up
- [ ] Receiving the max amount of petting I can get
- [ ] Personal lap warmer
- [ ] Gossiping with my meow-worker
- [ ] Trying to drink my owner's coffee while sitting on the laptop
- [ ] Accidentally adding bookmarks to my owner's computer because I want attention

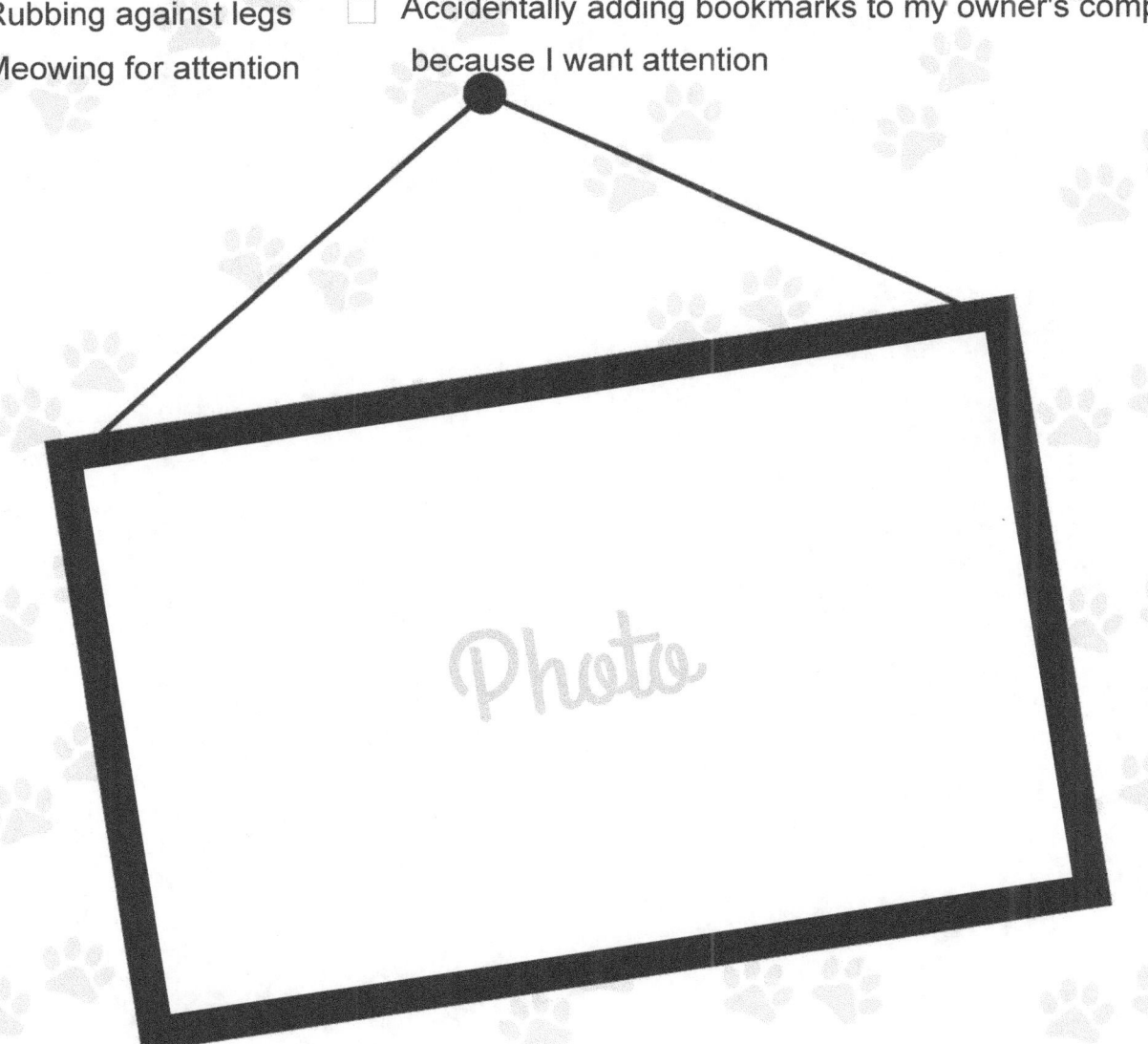

My Favorite Meow-Worker

Dear Meow-Worker, thanks for being my supportive four-legged "co-worker" at home today and I wanted to tell you that I love…

This is what it's like "working together" with you at home…

This is what I imagine you doing in the other room right now…

Today, you make me happy by…

Your favorite snack is…   Favorite place to sit is…   Your rating in the Snuggles department is… ☆☆☆☆☆

I am feeding you your favorite…   The times you made me laugh so hard are…   I love it when you…

I could use some more…   I could use a little less…   When you roll over, you…

On our "break time" from work, you love to…   Fave place to frantically run…

When I wash you, you…   My "support system" includes…   I find it funny when…

Some lessons I learned from knowing you are…   Favorite place to leave hairballs is….

Your favorite place to be scratched is….   The sound you make is…   Your favorite place to nap is…

You licked me this many times…   We snuggled this many times…   Favorite TV show is…

You were productive at "work" today by…   Your favorite toy to play with is…   You love to torture the…

Things I love

- [ ] Toys
- [ ] Cat nip
- [ ] Getting snuggles
- [ ] Purring
- [ ] Playtime
- [ ] Headbutting
- [ ] Laser pointers
- [ ] Treats for being cute
- [ ] Rubbing against legs
- [ ] Meowing for attention
- [ ] Sitting on the keyboard
- [ ] Licking my owner's neck
- [ ] "Meetings" with my new manager at home
- [ ] Waking my owner up
- [ ] Receiving the max amount of petting I can get
- [ ] Personal lap warmer
- [ ] Gossiping with my meow-worker
- [ ] Trying to drink my owner's coffee while sitting on the lapt
- [ ] Accidentally adding bookmarks to my owner's computer because I want attention

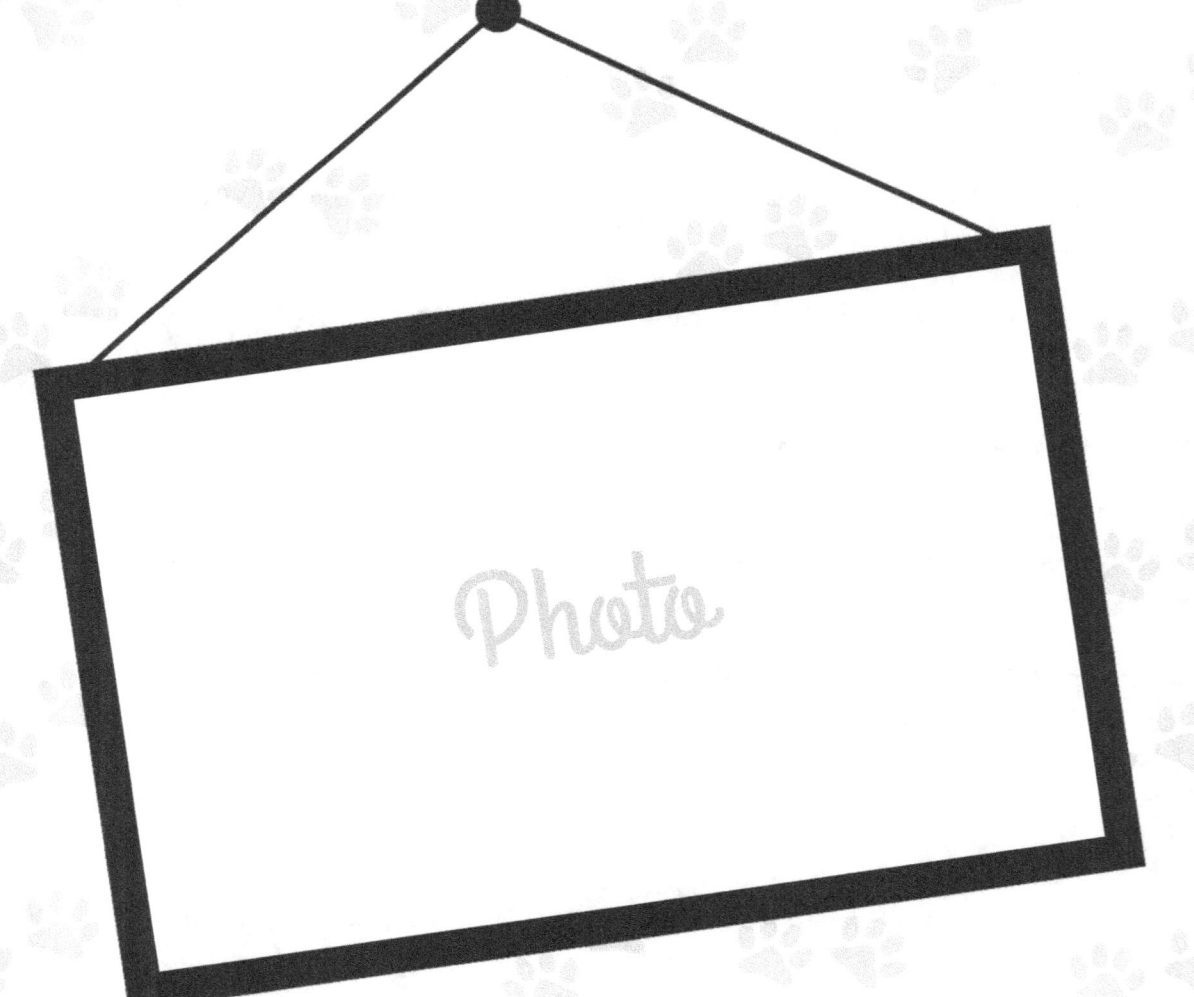

My Favorite Meow-Worker

Dear Meow-Worker, thanks for being my supportive four-legged "co-worker" at home today and I wanted to tell you that I love…

[ ]

This is what it's like "working together" with you at home…

[ ]

This is what I imagine you doing in the other room right now…

[ ]

Today, you make me happy by…

[ ]

Your favorite snack is…   Favorite place to sit is…   Your rating in the Snuggles department is… ☆ ☆ ☆ ☆ ☆

[ ]   [ ]

I am feeding you your favorite…   The times you made me laugh so hard are…   I love it when you…

[ ]   [ ]   [ ]

I could use some more…   I could use a little less…   When you roll over, you…

[ ]   [ ]   [ ]

On our "break time" from work, you love to…   Fave place to frantically run..

[ ]   [ ]

When I wash you, you…   My "support system" includes…   I find it funny when…

[ ]   [ ]   [ ]

Some lessons I learned from knowing you are…   Favorite place to leave hairballs is.

[ ]   [ ]

Your favorite place to be scratched is….   The sound you make is…   Your favorite place to nap is..

[ ]   [ ]   [ ]

You licked me this many times…   We snuggled this many times…   Favorite TV show is…

[ ]   [ ]   [ ]

You were productive at "work" today by…   Your favorite toy to play with is…   You love to torture the…

[ ]   [ ]   [ ]

Things I love

- [ ] Toys
- [ ] Cat nip
- [ ] Getting snuggles
- [ ] Purring
- [ ] Playtime
- [ ] Headbutting
- [ ] Laser pointers
- [ ] Treats for being cute
- [ ] Rubbing against legs
- [ ] Meowing for attention
- [ ] Sitting on the keyboard
- [ ] Licking my owner's neck
- [ ] "Meetings" with my new manager at home
- [ ] Waking my owner up
- [ ] Receiving the max amount of petting I can get
- [ ] Personal lap warmer
- [ ] Gossiping with my meow-worker
- [ ] Trying to drink my owner's coffee while sitting on the laptop
- [ ] Accidentally adding bookmarks to my owner's computer because I want attention

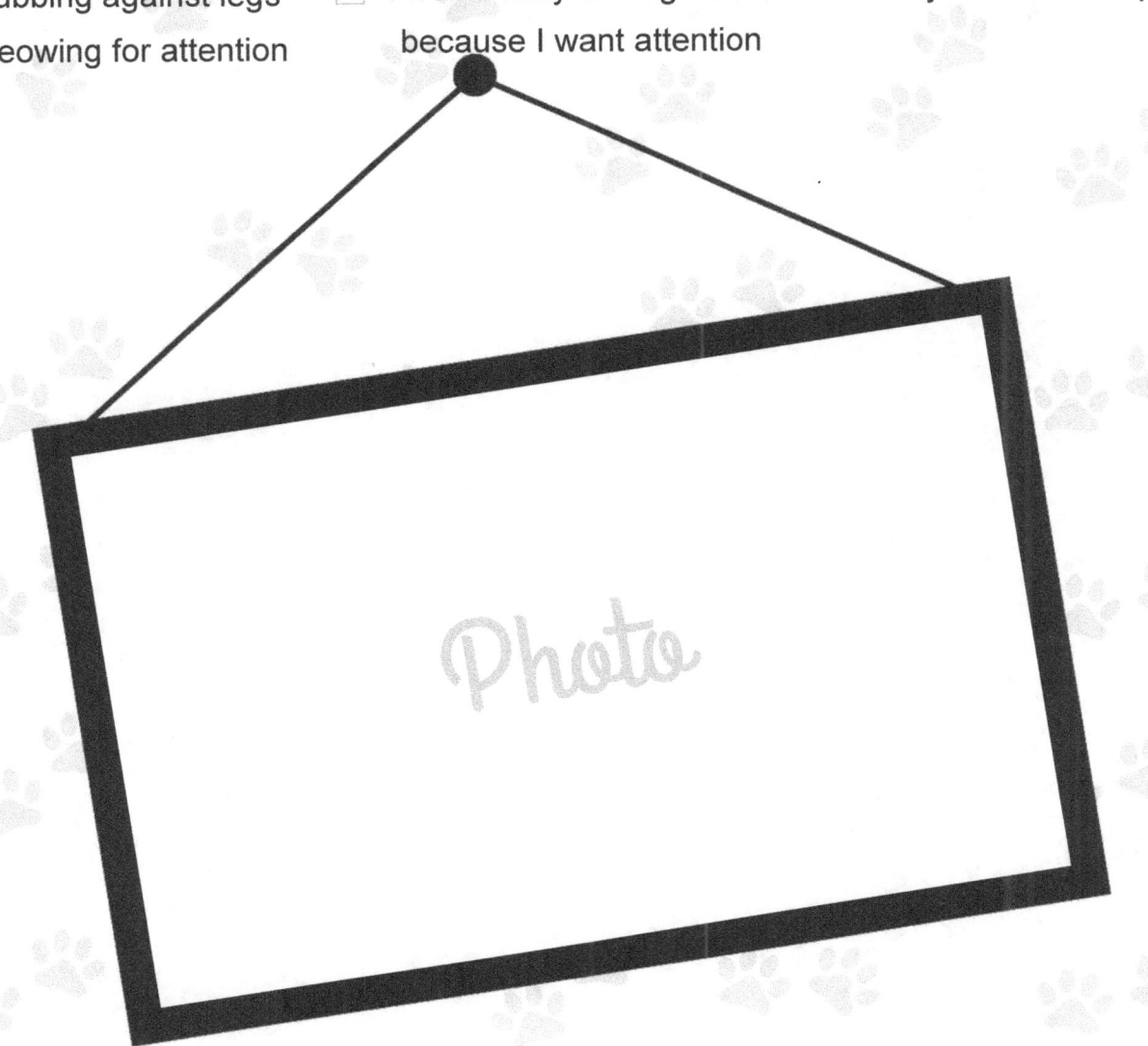

My Favorite Meow-Worker

Dear Meow-Worker, thanks for being my supportive four-legged "co-worker" at home today and I wanted to tell you that I love…

This is what it's like "working together" with you at home…

This is what I imagine you doing in the other room right now…

Today, you make me happy by…

Your favorite snack is… Favorite place to sit is… Your rating in the Snuggles department is… ☆☆☆☆☆

I am feeding you your favorite… The times you made me laugh so hard are… I love it when you…

I could use some more… I could use a little less… When you roll over, you…

On our "break time" from work, you love to… Fave place to frantically run…

When I wash you, you… My "support system" includes… I find it funny when…

Some lessons I learned from knowing you are… Favorite place to leave hairballs is….

Your favorite place to be scratched is…. The sound you make is… Your favorite place to nap is…

You licked me this many times… We snuggled this many times… Favorite TV show is…

You were productive at "work" today by… Your favorite toy to play with is… You love to torture the…

Things I love

- [ ] Toys
- [ ] Cat nip
- [ ] Getting snuggles
- [ ] Purring
- [ ] Playtime
- [ ] Headbutting
- [ ] Laser pointers
- [ ] Treats for being cute
- [ ] Rubbing against legs
- [ ] Meowing for attention
- [ ] Sitting on the keyboard
- [ ] Licking my owner's neck
- [ ] "Meetings" with my new manager at home
- [ ] Waking my owner up
- [ ] Receiving the max amount of petting I can get
- [ ] Personal lap warmer
- [ ] Gossiping with my meow-worker
- [ ] Trying to drink my owner's coffee while sitting on the lapt
- [ ] Accidentally adding bookmarks to my owner's computer because I want attention

My Favorite Meow-Worker

Dear Meow-Worker, thanks for being my supportive four-legged "co-worker" at home today and I wanted to tell you that I love…

[   ]

This is what it's like "working together" with you at home…

[   ]

This is what I imagine you doing in the other room right now…

[   ]

Today, you make me happy by…

[   ]

Your favorite snack is…	Favorite place to sit is…	Your rating in the Snuggles department is… ☆☆☆☆☆
I am feeding you your favorite…	The times you made me laugh so hard are…	I love it when you…
I could use some more…	I could use a little less…	When you roll over, you…
On our "break time" from work, you love to…		Fave place to frantically run…
When I wash you, you…	My "support system" includes…	I find it funny when…
Some lessons I learned from knowing you are…		Favorite place to leave hairballs is…
Your favorite place to be scratched is…	The sound you make is…	Your favorite place to nap is…
You licked me this many times…	We snuggled this many times…	Favorite TV show is…
You were productive at "work" today by…	Your favorite toy to play with is…	You love to torture the…

Things I love

- ☐ Toys
- ☐ Cat nip
- ☐ Getting snuggles
- ☐ Purring
- ☐ Playtime
- ☐ Headbutting
- ☐ Laser pointers
- ☐ Treats for being cute
- ☐ Rubbing against legs
- ☐ Meowing for attention
- ☐ Sitting on the keyboard
- ☐ Licking my owner's neck
- ☐ "Meetings" with my new manager at home
- ☐ Waking my owner up
- ☐ Receiving the max amount of petting I can get
- ☐ Personal lap warmer
- ☐ Gossiping with my meow-worker
- ☐ Trying to drink my owner's coffee while sitting on the laptop
- ☐ Accidentally adding bookmarks to my owner's computer because I want attention

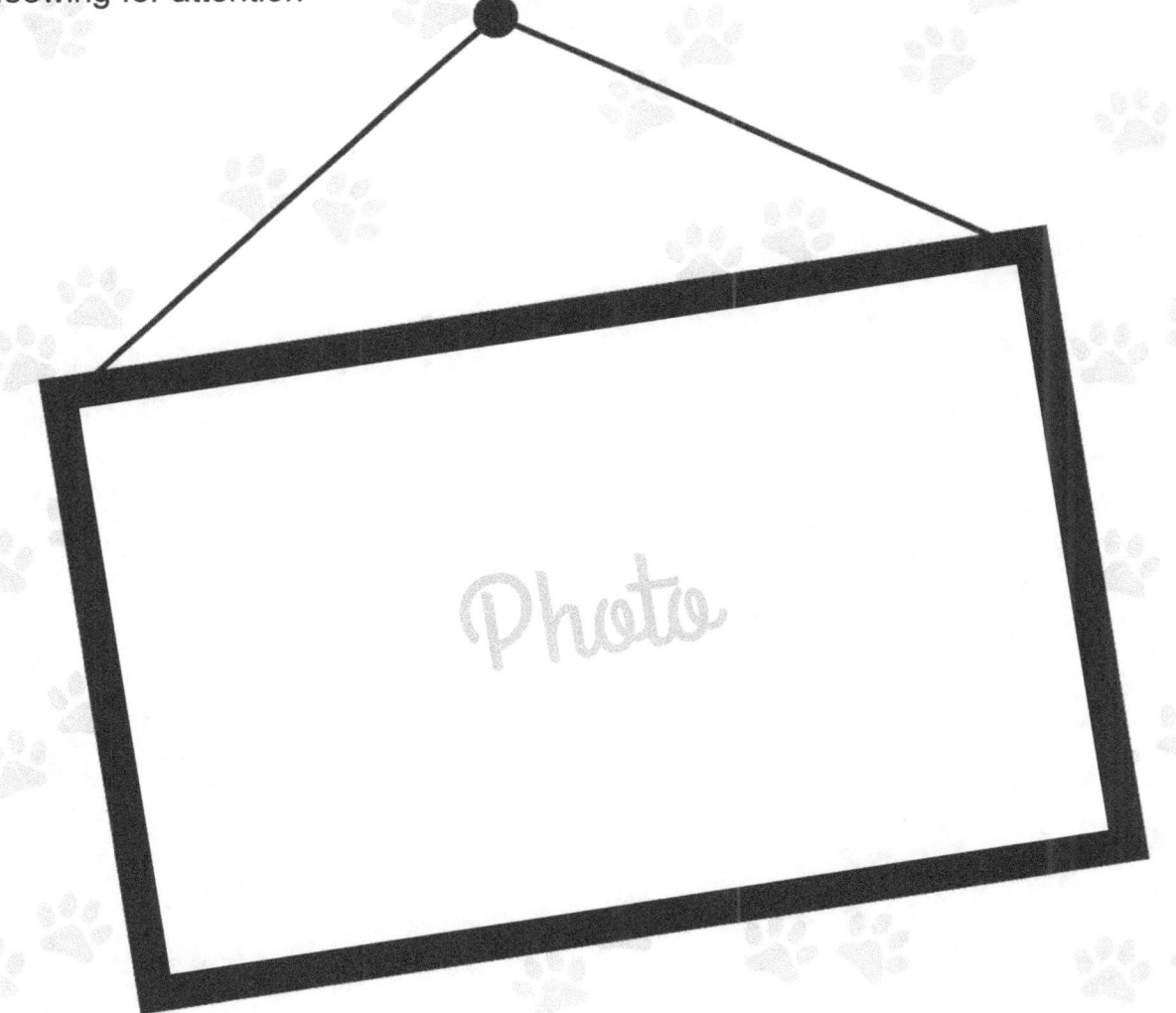

My Favorite Meow-Worker

Dear Meow-Worker, thanks for being my supportive four-legged "co-worker" at home today and I wanted to tell you that I love…

[   ]

This is what it's like "working together" with you at home…

[   ]

This is what I imagine you doing in the other room right now…

[   ]

Today, you make me happy by…

[   ]

Your favorite snack is…	Favorite place to sit is…	Your rating in the Snuggles department is… ☆☆☆☆☆
I am feeding you your favorite…	The times you made me laugh so hard are…	I love it when you…
I could use some more…	I could use a little less…	When you roll over, you…
On our "break time" from work, you love to…		Fave place to frantically run…
When I wash you, you…	My "support system" includes…	I find it funny when…
Some lessons I learned from knowing you are…		Favorite place to leave hairballs is….
Your favorite place to be scratched is….	The sound you make is…	Your favorite place to nap is…
You licked me this many times…	We snuggled this many times…	Favorite TV show is…
You were productive at "work" today by…	Your favorite toy to play with is…	You love to torture the…

Things I love

- [ ] Toys
- [ ] Cat nip
- [ ] Getting snuggles
- [ ] Purring
- [ ] Playtime
- [ ] Headbutting
- [ ] Laser pointers
- [ ] Treats for being cute
- [ ] Rubbing against legs
- [ ] Meowing for attention
- [ ] Sitting on the keyboard
- [ ] Licking my owner's neck
- [ ] "Meetings" with my new manager at home
- [ ] Waking my owner up
- [ ] Receiving the max amount of petting I can get
- [ ] Personal lap warmer
- [ ] Gossiping with my meow-worker
- [ ] Trying to drink my owner's coffee while sitting on the lapt
- [ ] Accidentally adding bookmarks to my owner's computer because I want attention

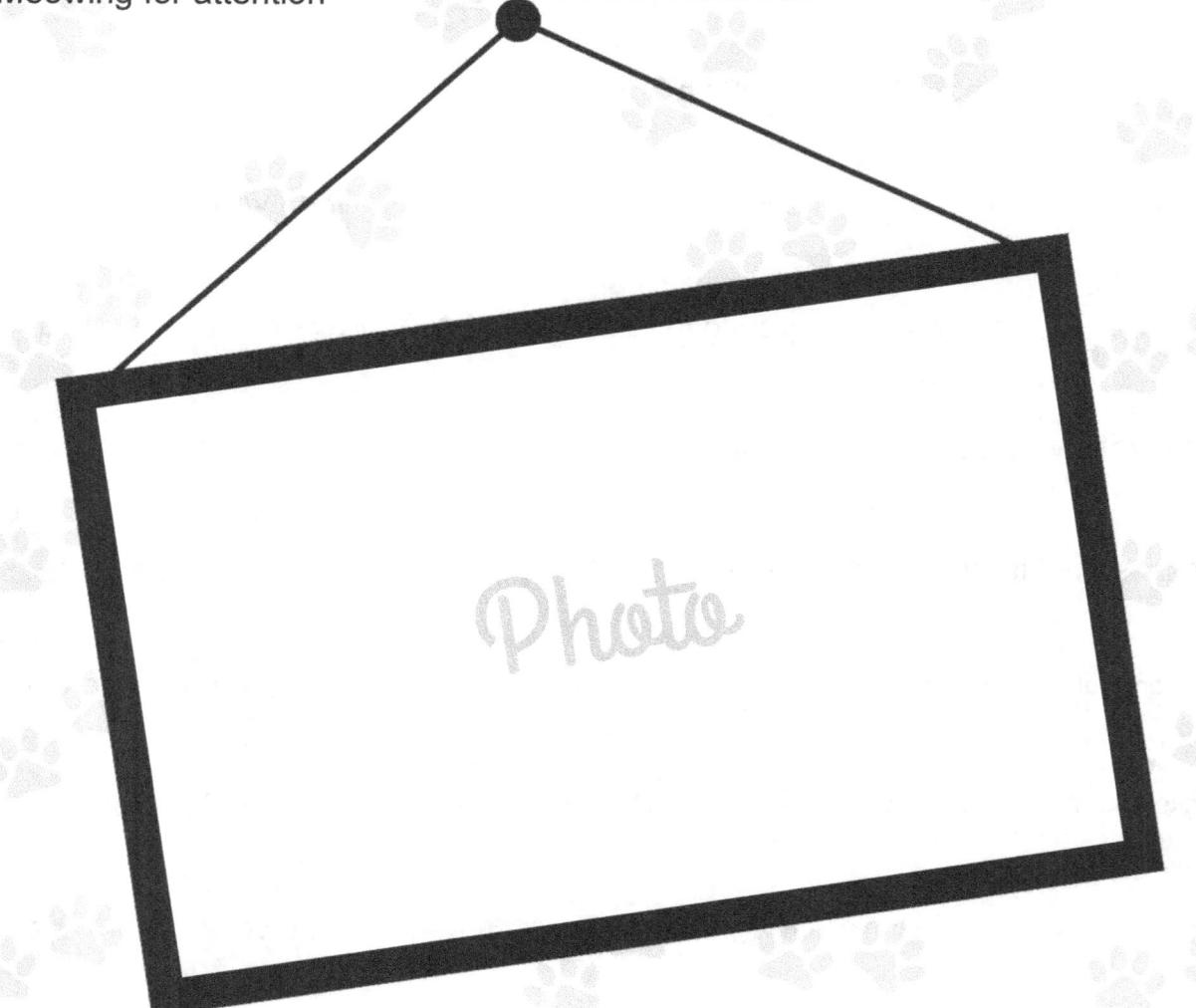

My Favorite Meow-Worker

Dear Meow-Worker, thanks for being my supportive four-legged "co-worker" at home today and I wanted to tell you that I love…

This is what it's like "working together" with you at home…

This is what I imagine you doing in the other room right now…

Today, you make me happy by…

Your favorite snack is…

Favorite place to sit is…

Your rating in the Snuggles department is… ☆☆☆☆☆

I am feeding you your favorite…

The times you made me laugh so hard are…

I love it when you…

I could use some more…

I could use a little less…

When you roll over, you…

On our "break time" from work, you love to…

Fave place to frantically run…

When I wash you, you…

My "support system" includes…

I find it funny when…

Some lessons I learned from knowing you are…

Favorite place to leave hairballs is…

Your favorite place to be scratched is…

The sound you make is…

Your favorite place to nap is…

You licked me this many times…

We snuggled this many times…

Favorite TV show is…

You were productive at "work" today by…

Your favorite toy to play with is…

You love to torture the…

Things I love

- [ ] Toys
- [ ] Cat nip
- [ ] Getting snuggles
- [ ] Purring
- [ ] Playtime
- [ ] Headbutting
- [ ] Laser pointers
- [ ] Treats for being cute
- [ ] Rubbing against legs
- [ ] Meowing for attention
- [ ] Sitting on the keyboard
- [ ] Licking my owner's neck
- [ ] "Meetings" with my new manager at home
- [ ] Waking my owner up
- [ ] Receiving the max amount of petting I can get
- [ ] Personal lap warmer
- [ ] Gossiping with my meow-worker
- [ ] Trying to drink my owner's coffee while sitting on the laptop
- [ ] Accidentally adding bookmarks to my owner's computer because I want attention

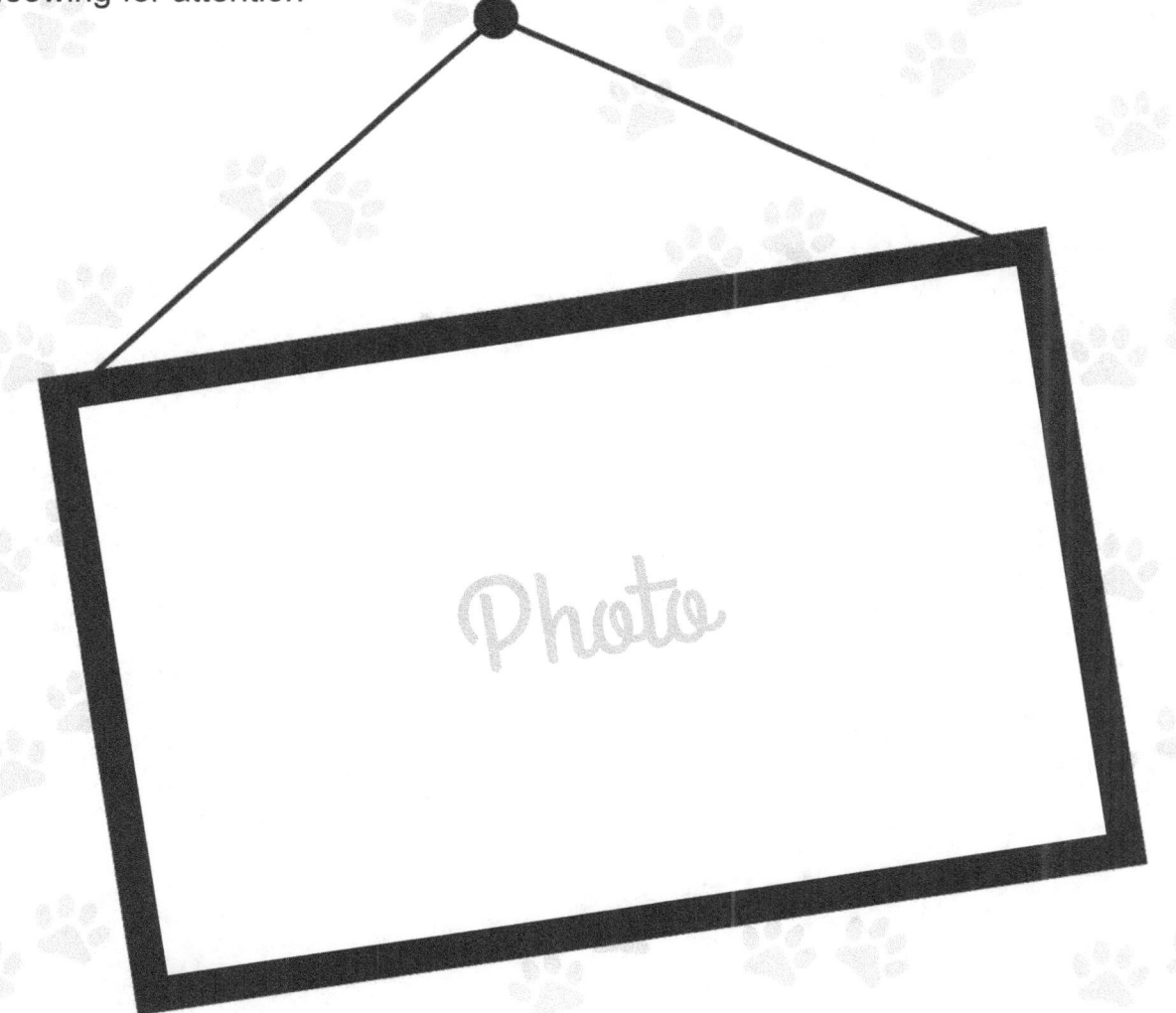

My Favorite Meow-Worker

Dear Meow-Worker, thanks for being my supportive four-legged "co-worker" at home today and I wanted to tell you that I love…

This is what it's like "working together" with you at home…

This is what I imagine you doing in the other room right now…

Today, you make me happy by…

Your favorite snack is… | Favorite place to sit is… | Your rating in the Snuggles department is… ☆☆☆☆☆

I am feeding you your favorite… | The times you made me laugh so hard are… | I love it when you…

I could use some more… | I could use a little less… | When you roll over, you…

On our "break time" from work, you love to… | | Fave place to frantically run…

When I wash you, you… | My "support system" includes… | I find it funny when…

Some lessons I learned from knowing you are… | | Favorite place to leave hairballs is….

Your favorite place to be scratched is…. | The sound you make is… | Your favorite place to nap is…

You licked me this many times… | We snuggled this many times… | Favorite TV show is…

You were productive at "work" today by… | Your favorite toy to play with is… | You love to torture the…

Things I love

- [ ] Toys
- [ ] Cat nip
- [ ] Getting snuggles
- [ ] Purring
- [ ] Playtime
- [ ] Headbutting
- [ ] Laser pointers
- [ ] Treats for being cute
- [ ] Rubbing against legs
- [ ] Meowing for attention
- [ ] Sitting on the keyboard
- [ ] Licking my owner's neck
- [ ] "Meetings" with my new manager at home
- [ ] Waking my owner up
- [ ] Receiving the max amount of petting I can get
- [ ] Personal lap warmer
- [ ] Gossiping with my meow-worker
- [ ] Trying to drink my owner's coffee while sitting on the lapt
- [ ] Accidentally adding bookmarks to my owner's computer because I want attention

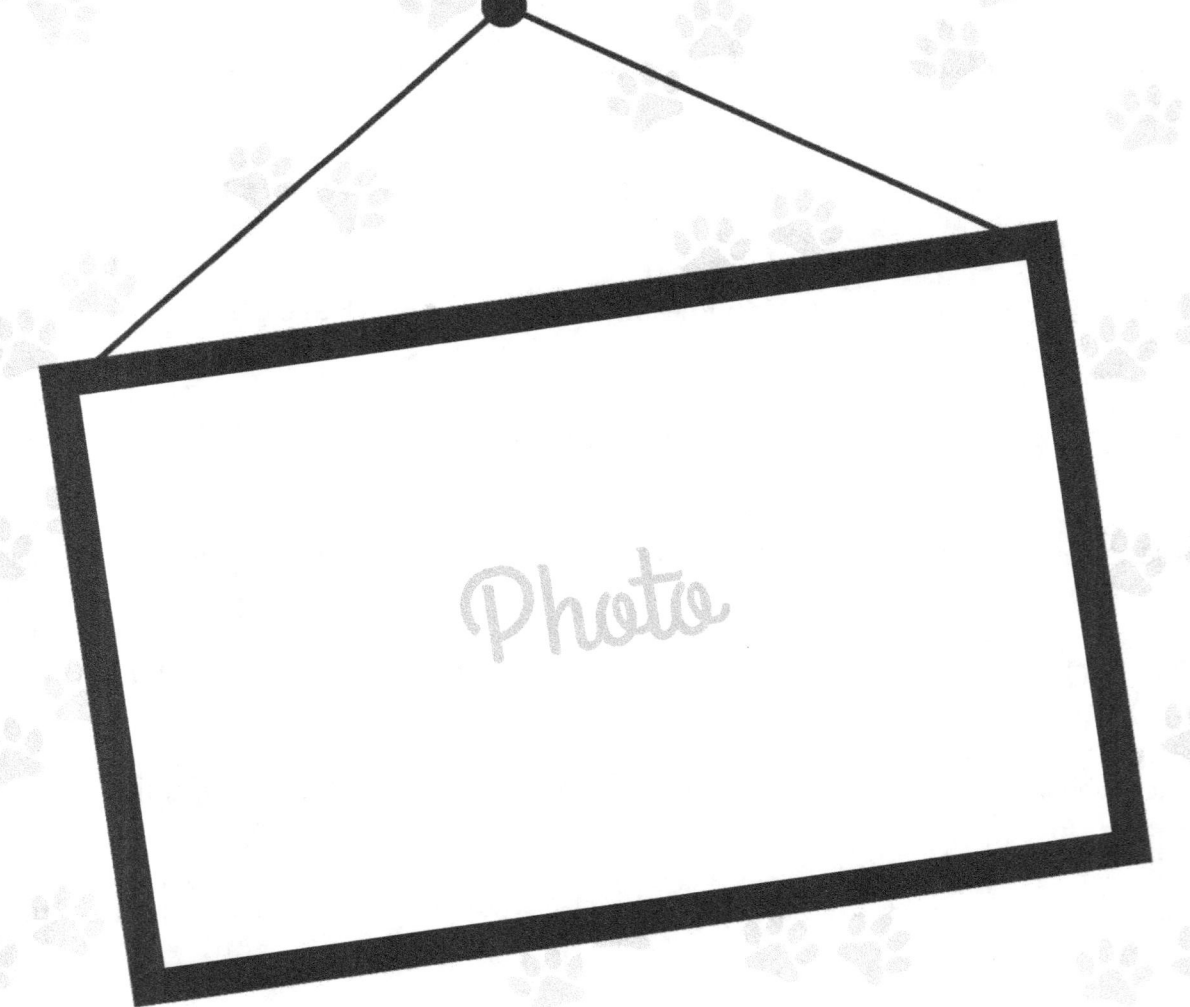

My Favorite Meow-Worker

Dear Meow-Worker, thanks for being my supportive four-legged "co-worker" at home today and I wanted to tell you that I love…

This is what it's like "working together" with you at home…

This is what I imagine you doing in the other room right now…

Today, you make me happy by…

Your favorite snack is…   Favorite place to sit is…   Your rating in the Snuggles department is… ☆☆☆☆☆

I am feeding you your favorite…   The times you made me laugh so hard are…   I love it when you…

I could use some more…   I could use a little less…   When you roll over, you…

On our "break time" from work, you love to…   Fave place to frantically run..

When I wash you, you…   My "support system" includes…   I find it funny when…

Some lessons I learned from knowing you are…   Favorite place to leave hairballs is..

Your favorite place to be scratched is….The sound you make is…   Your favorite place to nap is..

You licked me this many times…   We snuggled this many times…   Favorite TV show is…

You were productive at "work" today by…Your favorite toy to play with is…   You love to torture the…

Things I love

- [ ] Toys
- [ ] Cat nip
- [ ] Getting snuggles
- [ ] Purring
- [ ] Playtime
- [ ] Headbutting
- [ ] Laser pointers
- [ ] Treats for being cute
- [ ] Rubbing against legs
- [ ] Meowing for attention
- [ ] Sitting on the keyboard
- [ ] Licking my owner's neck
- [ ] "Meetings" with my new manager at home
- [ ] Waking my owner up
- [ ] Receiving the max amount of petting I can get
- [ ] Personal lap warmer
- [ ] Gossiping with my meow-worker
- [ ] Trying to drink my owner's coffee while sitting on the laptop
- [ ] Accidentally adding bookmarks to my owner's computer because I want attention

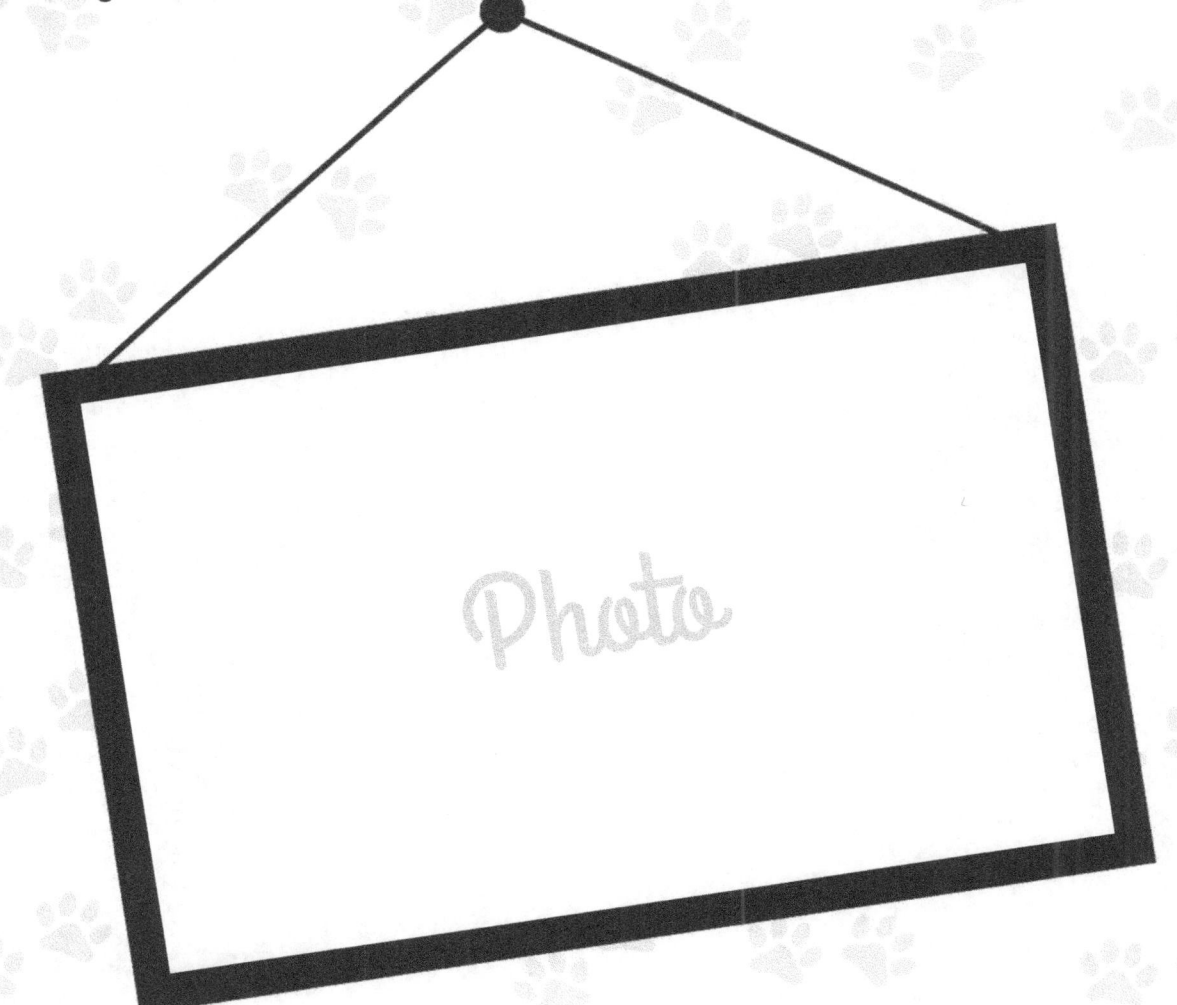

My Favorite Meow-Worker

Dear Meow-Worker, thanks for being my supportive four-legged "co-worker" at home today and I wanted to tell you that I love…

This is what it's like "working together" with you at home…

This is what I imagine you doing in the other room right now…

Today, you make me happy by…

Your favorite snack is… | Favorite place to sit is… | Your rating in the Snuggles department is… ☆☆☆☆☆

I am feeding you your favorite… | The times you made me laugh so hard are… | I love it when you…

I could use some more… | I could use a little less… | When you roll over, you…

On our "break time" from work, you love to… | | Fave place to frantically run…

When I wash you, you… | My "support system" includes… | I find it funny when…

Some lessons I learned from knowing you are… | | Favorite place to leave hairballs is….

Your favorite place to be scratched is…. | The sound you make is… | Your favorite place to nap is…

You licked me this many times… | We snuggled this many times… | Favorite TV show is…

You were productive at "work" today by… | Your favorite toy to play with is… | You love to torture the…

Things I love

- ☐ Toys
- ☐ Cat nip
- ☐ Getting snuggles
- ☐ Purring
- ☐ Playtime
- ☐ Headbutting
- ☐ Laser pointers
- ☐ Treats for being cute
- ☐ Rubbing against legs
- ☐ Meowing for attention
- ☐ Sitting on the keyboard
- ☐ Licking my owner's neck
- ☐ "Meetings" with my new manager at home
- ☐ Waking my owner up
- ☐ Receiving the max amount of petting I can get
- ☐ Personal lap warmer
- ☐ Gossiping with my meow-worker
- ☐ Trying to drink my owner's coffee while sitting on the lapt
- ☐ Accidentally adding bookmarks to my owner's computer because I want attention

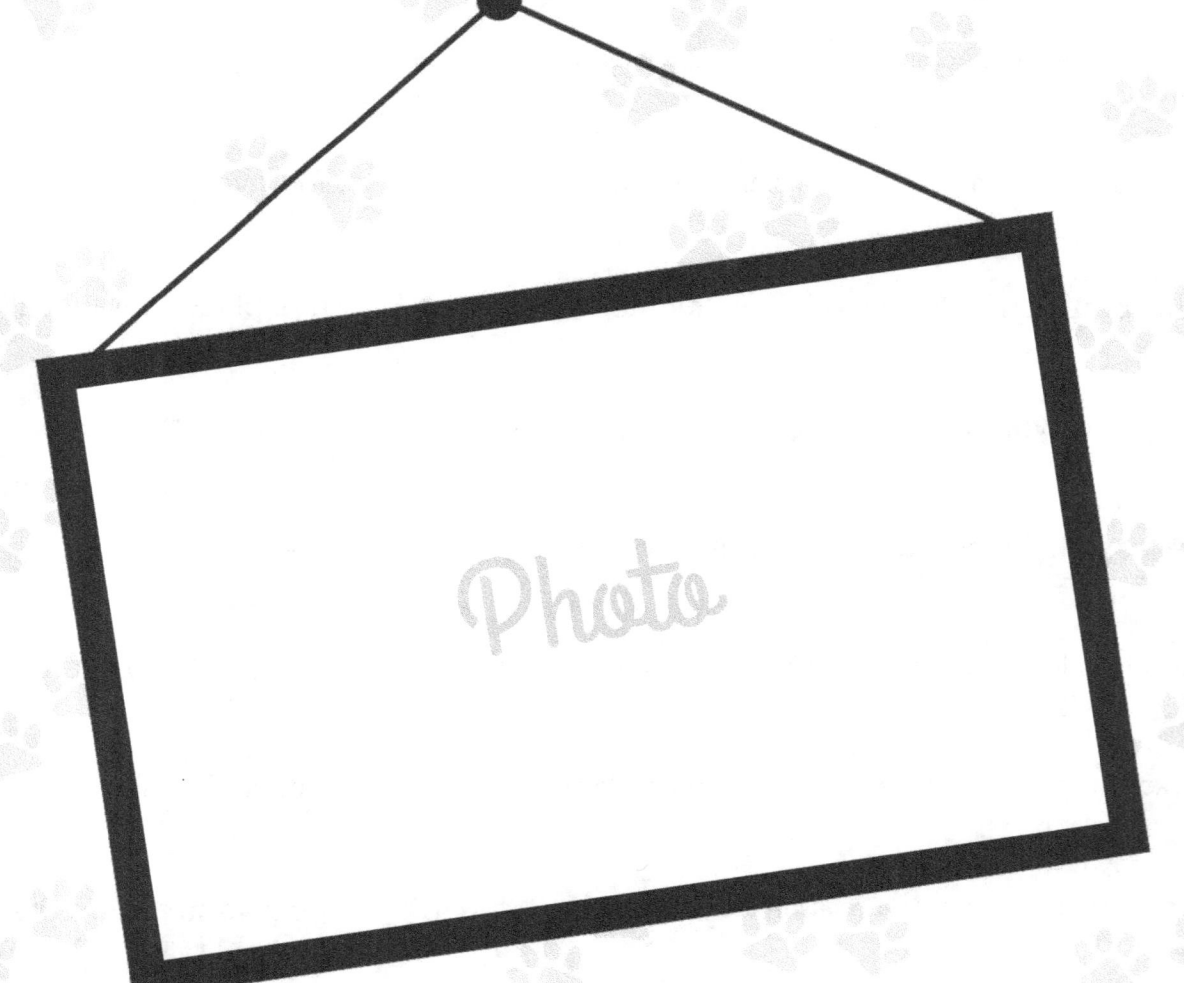

My Favorite Meow-Worker

Dear Meow-Worker, thanks for being my supportive four-legged "co-worker" at home today and I wanted to tell you that I love…

[   ]

This is what it's like "working together" with you at home…

[   ]

This is what I imagine you doing in the other room right now…

[   ]

Today, you make me happy by…

[   ]

Your favorite snack is…	Favorite place to sit is…	Your rating in the Snuggles department is… ☆☆☆☆☆
I am feeding you your favorite…	The times you made me laugh so hard are…	I love it when you…
I could use some more…	I could use a little less…	When you roll over, you…
On our "break time" from work, you love to…		Fave place to frantically run…
When I wash you, you…	My "support system" includes…	I find it funny when…
Some lessons I learned from knowing you are…		Favorite place to leave hairballs is
Your favorite place to be scratched is…	The sound you make is…	Your favorite place to nap is…
You licked me this many times…	We snuggled this many times…	Favorite TV show is…
You were productive at "work" today by…	Your favorite toy to play with is…	You love to torture the…

Things I love

- ☐ Toys
- ☐ Cat nip
- ☐ Getting snuggles
- ☐ Purring
- ☐ Playtime
- ☐ Headbutting
- ☐ Laser pointers
- ☐ Treats for being cute
- ☐ Rubbing against legs
- ☐ Meowing for attention
- ☐ Sitting on the keyboard
- ☐ Licking my owner's neck
- ☐ "Meetings" with my new manager at home
- ☐ Waking my owner up
- ☐ Receiving the max amount of petting I can get
- ☐ Personal lap warmer
- ☐ Gossiping with my meow-worker
- ☐ Trying to drink my owner's coffee while sitting on the laptop
- ☐ Accidentally adding bookmarks to my owner's computer because I want attention

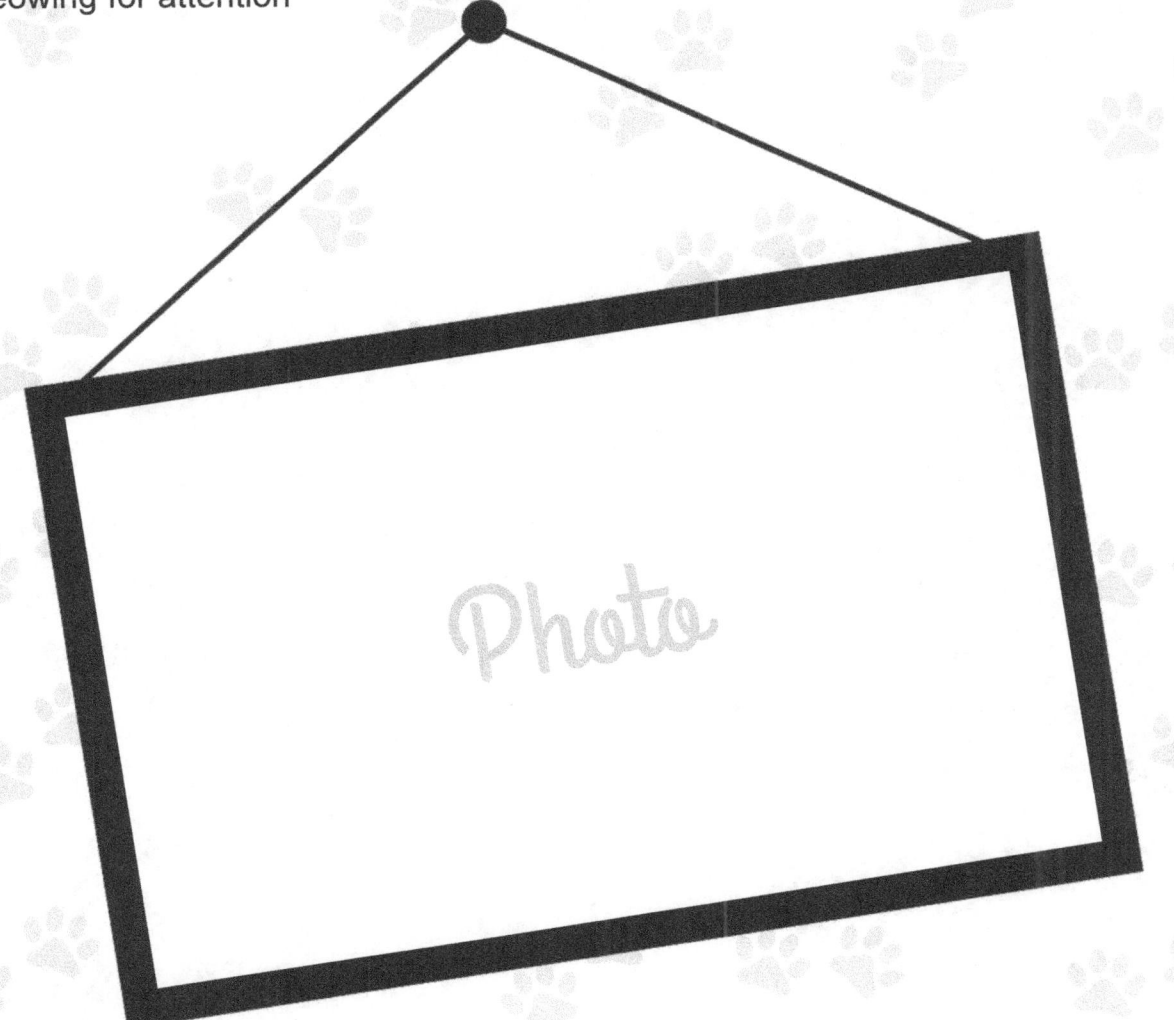

My Favorite Meow-Worker

Dear Meow-Worker, thanks for being my supportive four-legged "co-worker" at home today and I wanted to tell you that I love…

This is what it's like "working together" with you at home…

This is what I imagine you doing in the other room right now…

Today, you make me happy by…

Your favorite snack is…   Favorite place to sit is…   Your rating in the Snuggles department is… ☆☆☆☆☆

I am feeding you your favorite…   The times you made me laugh so hard are…   I love it when you…

I could use some more…   I could use a little less…   When you roll over, you…

On our "break time" from work, you love to…   Fave place to frantically run…

When I wash you, you…   My "support system" includes…   I find it funny when…

Some lessons I learned from knowing you are…   Favorite place to leave hairballs is….

Your favorite place to be scratched is….   The sound you make is…   Your favorite place to nap is…

You licked me this many times…   We snuggled this many times…   Favorite TV show is…

You were productive at "work" today by…   Your favorite toy to play with is…   You love to torture the…

Things I love

- ☐ Toys
- ☐ Cat nip
- ☐ Getting snuggles
- ☐ Purring
- ☐ Playtime
- ☐ Headbutting
- ☐ Laser pointers
- ☐ Treats for being cute
- ☐ Rubbing against legs
- ☐ Meowing for attention

- ☐ Sitting on the keyboard
- ☐ Licking my owner's neck
- ☐ "Meetings" with my new manager at home
- ☐ Waking my owner up
- ☐ Receiving the max amount of petting I can get
- ☐ Personal lap warmer
- ☐ Gossiping with my meow-worker
- ☐ Trying to drink my owner's coffee while sitting on the laptop
- ☐ Accidentally adding bookmarks to my owner's computer because I want attention

Photo

My Favorite Meow-Worker

Dear Meow-Worker, thanks for being my supportive four-legged "co-worker" at home today and I wanted to tell you that I love…

This is what it's like "working together" with you at home…

This is what I imagine you doing in the other room right now…

Today, you make me happy by…

Your favorite snack is… Favorite place to sit is… Your rating in the Snuggles department is… ☆☆☆☆☆

I am feeding you your favorite… The times you made me laugh so hard are… I love it when you…

I could use some more… I could use a little less… When you roll over, you…

On our "break time" from work, you love to… Fave place to frantically run..

When I wash you, you… My "support system" includes… I find it funny when…

Some lessons I learned from knowing you are… Favorite place to leave hairballs is.

Your favorite place to be scratched is…. The sound you make is… Your favorite place to nap is..

You licked me this many times… We snuggled this many times… Favorite TV show is…

You were productive at "work" today by… Your favorite toy to play with is… You love to torture the…

Things I love

- ☑ Toys
- ☐ Cat nip
- ☐ Getting snuggles
- ☐ Purring
- ☐ Playtime
- ☐ Headbutting
- ☐ Laser pointers
- ☐ Treats for being cute
- ☐ Rubbing against legs
- ☐ Meowing for attention
- ☐ Sitting on the keyboard
- ☐ Licking my owner's neck
- ☐ "Meetings" with my new manager at home
- ☐ Waking my owner up
- ☐ Receiving the max amount of petting I can get
- ☐ Personal lap warmer
- ☐ Gossiping with my meow-worker
- ☐ Trying to drink my owner's coffee while sitting on the laptop
- ☐ Accidentally adding bookmarks to my owner's computer because I want attention

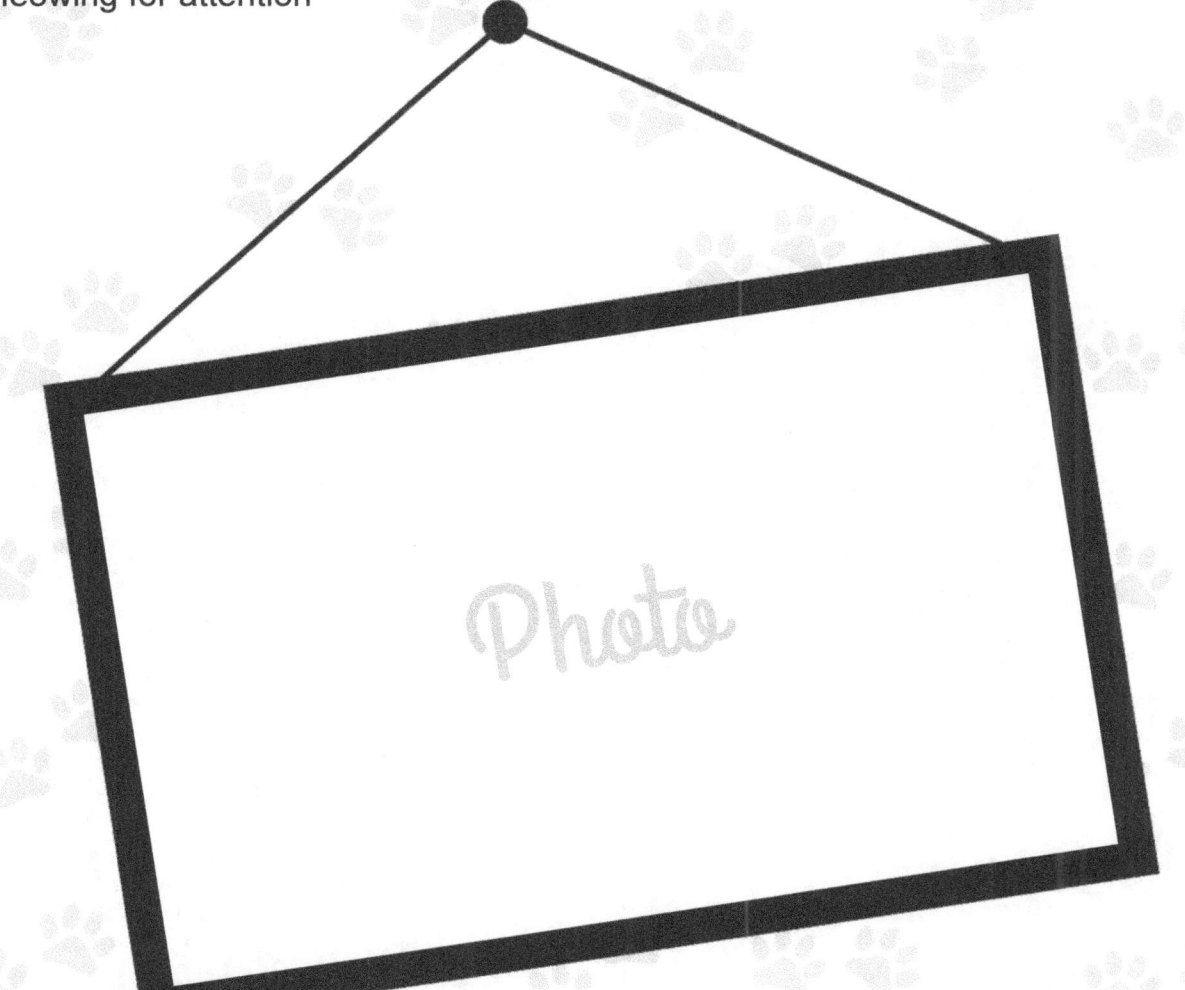

My Favorite Meow-Worker

Dear Meow-Worker, thanks for being my supportive four-legged "co-worker" at home today and I wanted to tell you that I love…

___

This is what it's like "working together" with you at home…

___

This is what I imagine you doing in the other room right now…

___

Today, you make me happy by…

___

Your favorite snack is... | Favorite place to sit is… | Your rating in the Snuggles department is… ☆☆☆☆☆

I am feeding you your favorite… | The times you made me laugh so hard are… | I love it when you…

I could use some more… | I could use a little less… | When you roll over, you…

On our "break time" from work, you love to… | | Fave place to frantically run…

When I wash you, you… | My "support system" includes… | I find it funny when…

Some lessons I learned from knowing you are… | | Favorite place to leave hairballs is….

Your favorite place to be scratched is…. | The sound you make is… | Your favorite place to nap is…

You licked me this many times… | We snuggled this many times… | Favorite TV show is…

You were productive at "work" today by… | Your favorite toy to play with is… | You love to torture the…

Things I love

- ☐ Toys
- ☐ Cat nip
- ☐ Getting snuggles
- ☐ Purring
- ☐ Playtime
- ☐ Headbutting
- ☐ Laser pointers
- ☐ Treats for being cute
- ☐ Rubbing against legs
- ☐ Meowing for attention
- ☐ Sitting on the keyboard
- ☐ Licking my owner's neck
- ☐ "Meetings" with my new manager at home
- ☐ Waking my owner up
- ☐ Receiving the max amount of petting I can get
- ☐ Personal lap warmer
- ☐ Gossiping with my meow-worker
- ☐ Trying to drink my owner's coffee while sitting on the lapt
- ☐ Accidentally adding bookmarks to my owner's computer because I want attention

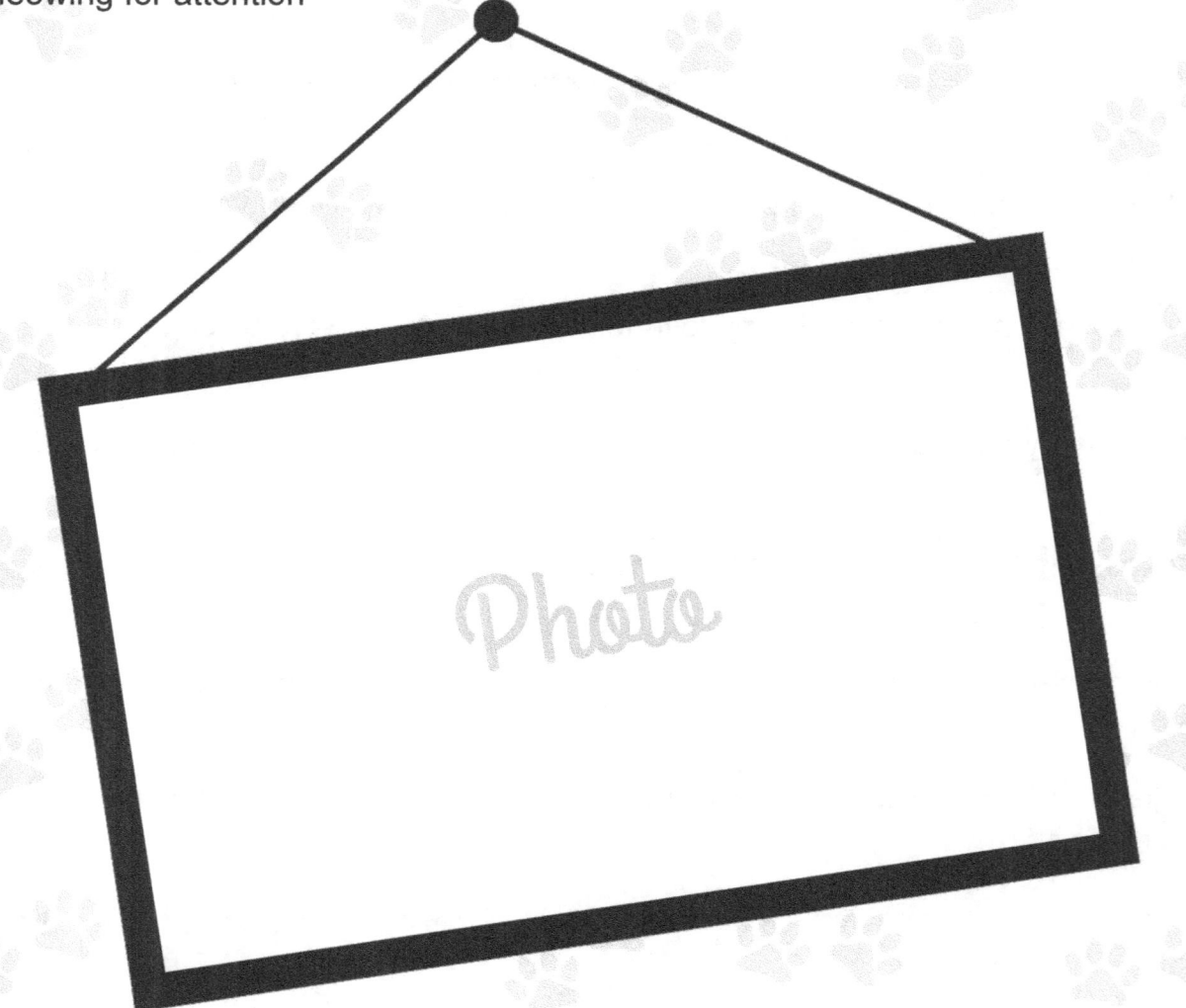

My Favorite Meow-Worker

Dear Meow-Worker, thanks for being my supportive four-legged "co-worker" at home today and I wanted to tell you that I love…

[ ]

This is what it's like "working together" with you at home…

[ ]

This is what I imagine you doing in the other room right now…

[ ]

Today, you make me happy by…

[ ]

Your favorite snack is…	Favorite place to sit is…	Your rating in the Snuggles department is… ☆☆☆☆☆
I am feeding you your favorite…	The times you made me laugh so hard are…	I love it when you…
I could use some more…	I could use a little less…	When you roll over, you…
On our "break time" from work, you love to…		Fave place to frantically run…
When I wash you, you…	My "support system" includes…	I find it funny when…
Some lessons I learned from knowing you are…		Favorite place to leave hairballs is
Your favorite place to be scratched is…	The sound you make is…	Your favorite place to nap is…
You licked me this many times…	We snuggled this many times…	Favorite TV show is…
You were productive at "work" today by…	Your favorite toy to play with is…	You love to torture the…

Things I love

- ☐ Toys
- ☐ Cat nip
- ☐ Getting snuggles
- ☐ Purring
- ☐ Playtime
- ☐ Headbutting
- ☐ Laser pointers
- ☐ Treats for being cute
- ☐ Rubbing against legs
- ☐ Meowing for attention
- ☐ Sitting on the keyboard
- ☐ Licking my owner's neck
- ☐ "Meetings" with my new manager at home
- ☐ Waking my owner up
- ☐ Receiving the max amount of petting I can get
- ☐ Personal lap warmer
- ☐ Gossiping with my meow-worker
- ☐ Trying to drink my owner's coffee while sitting on the laptop
- ☐ Accidentally adding bookmarks to my owner's computer because I want attention

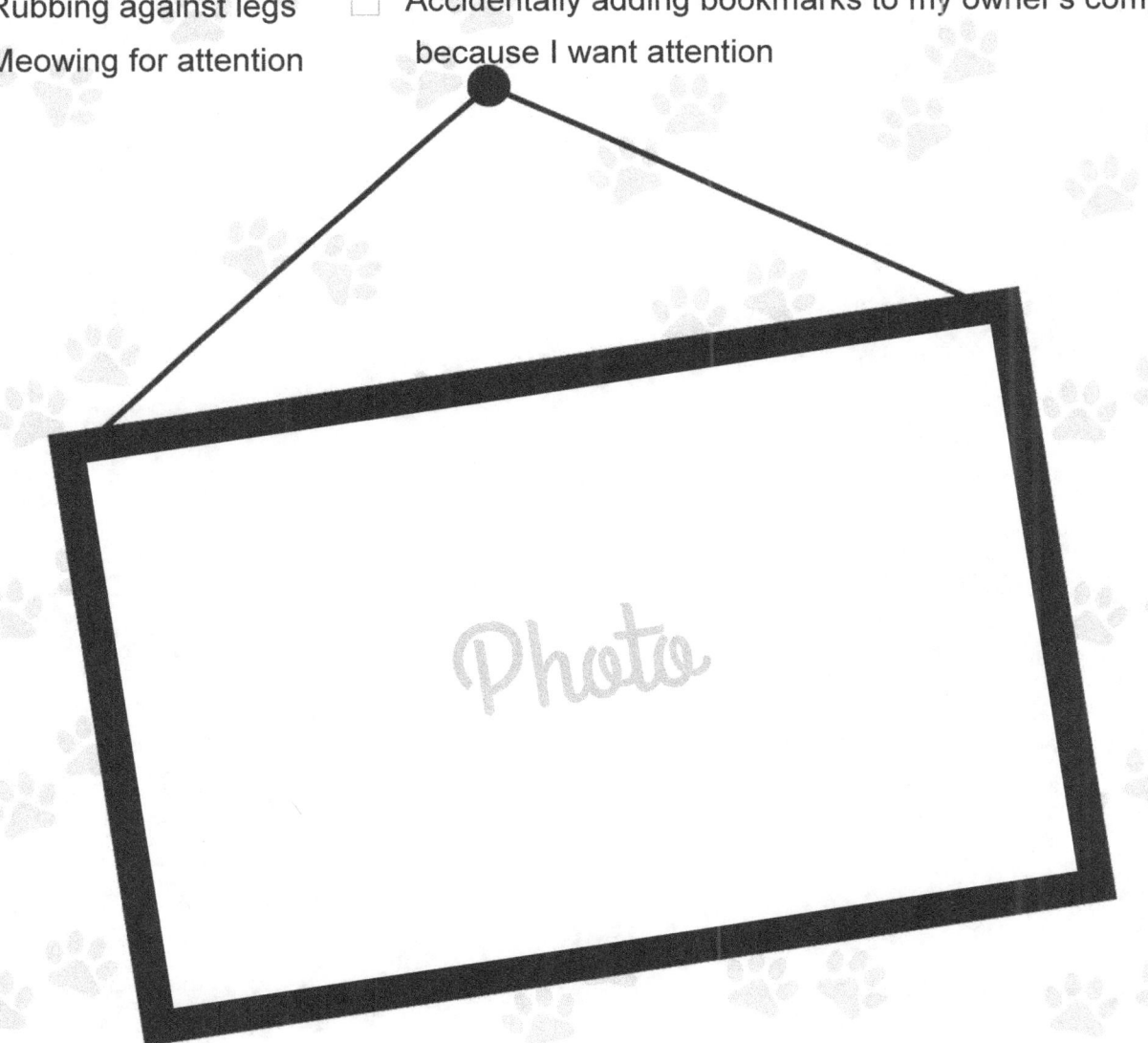

My Favorite Meow-Worker

Dear Meow-Worker, thanks for being my supportive four-legged "co-worker" at home today and I wanted to tell you that I love…

This is what it's like "working together" with you at home…

This is what I imagine you doing in the other room right now…

Today, you make me happy by…

Your favorite snack is…

Favorite place to sit is…

Your rating in the Snuggles department is… ☆☆☆☆☆

I am feeding you your favorite…

The times you made me laugh so hard are…

I love it when you…

I could use some more…

I could use a little less…

When you roll over, you…

On our "break time" from work, you love to…

Fave place to frantically run…

When I wash you, you…

My "support system" includes…

I find it funny when…

Some lessons I learned from knowing you are…

Favorite place to leave hairballs is….

Your favorite place to be scratched is….

The sound you make is…

Your favorite place to nap is…

You licked me this many times…

We snuggled this many times…

Favorite TV show is…

You were productive at "work" today by…

Your favorite toy to play with is…

You love to torture the…

Things I love

- ☐ Toys
- ☐ Cat nip
- ☐ Getting snuggles
- ☐ Purring
- ☐ Playtime
- ☐ Headbutting
- ☐ Laser pointers
- ☐ Treats for being cute
- ☐ Rubbing against legs
- ☐ Meowing for attention
- ☐ Sitting on the keyboard
- ☐ Licking my owner's neck
- ☐ "Meetings" with my new manager at home
- ☐ Waking my owner up
- ☐ Receiving the max amount of petting I can get
- ☐ Personal lap warmer
- ☐ Gossiping with my meow-worker
- ☐ Trying to drink my owner's coffee while sitting on the laptop
- ☐ Accidentally adding bookmarks to my owner's computer because I want attention

Photo

My Favorite Meow-Worker

Dear Meow-Worker, thanks for being my supportive four-legged "co-worker" at home today and I wanted to tell you that I love…

[ ]

This is what it's like "working together" with you at home…

[ ]

This is what I imagine you doing in the other room right now…

[ ]

Today, you make me happy by…

[ ]

Your favorite snack is… | Favorite place to sit is… | Your rating in the Snuggles department is… ☆☆☆☆☆

[ ] | [ ] |

I am feeding you your favorite… | The times you made me laugh so hard are… | I love it when you…

[ ] | [ ] | [ ]

I could use some more… | I could use a little less… | When you roll over, you…

[ ] | [ ] | [ ]

On our "break time" from work, you love to… | | Fave place to frantically run..

[ ] | | [ ]

When I wash you, you… | My "support system" includes… | I find it funny when…

[ ] | [ ] | [ ]

Some lessons I learned from knowing you are… | | Favorite place to leave hairballs is.

[ ] | | [ ]

Your favorite place to be scratched is…. | The sound you make is… | Your favorite place to nap is..

[ ] | [ ] | [ ]

You licked me this many times… | We snuggled this many times… | Favorite TV show is…

[ ] | [ ] | [ ]

You were productive at "work" today by… | Your favorite toy to play with is… | You love to torture the…

[ ] | [ ] | [ ]

Things I love

- ☐ Toys
- ☐ Cat nip
- ☐ Getting snuggles
- ☐ Purring
- ☐ Playtime
- ☐ Headbutting
- ☐ Laser pointers
- ☐ Treats for being cute
- ☐ Rubbing against legs
- ☐ Meowing for attention

- ☐ Sitting on the keyboard
- ☐ Licking my owner's neck
- ☐ "Meetings" with my new manager at home
- ☐ Waking my owner up
- ☐ Receiving the max amount of petting I can get
- ☐ Personal lap warmer
- ☐ Gossiping with my meow-worker
- ☐ Trying to drink my owner's coffee while sitting on the laptop
- ☐ Accidentally adding bookmarks to my owner's computer because I want attention

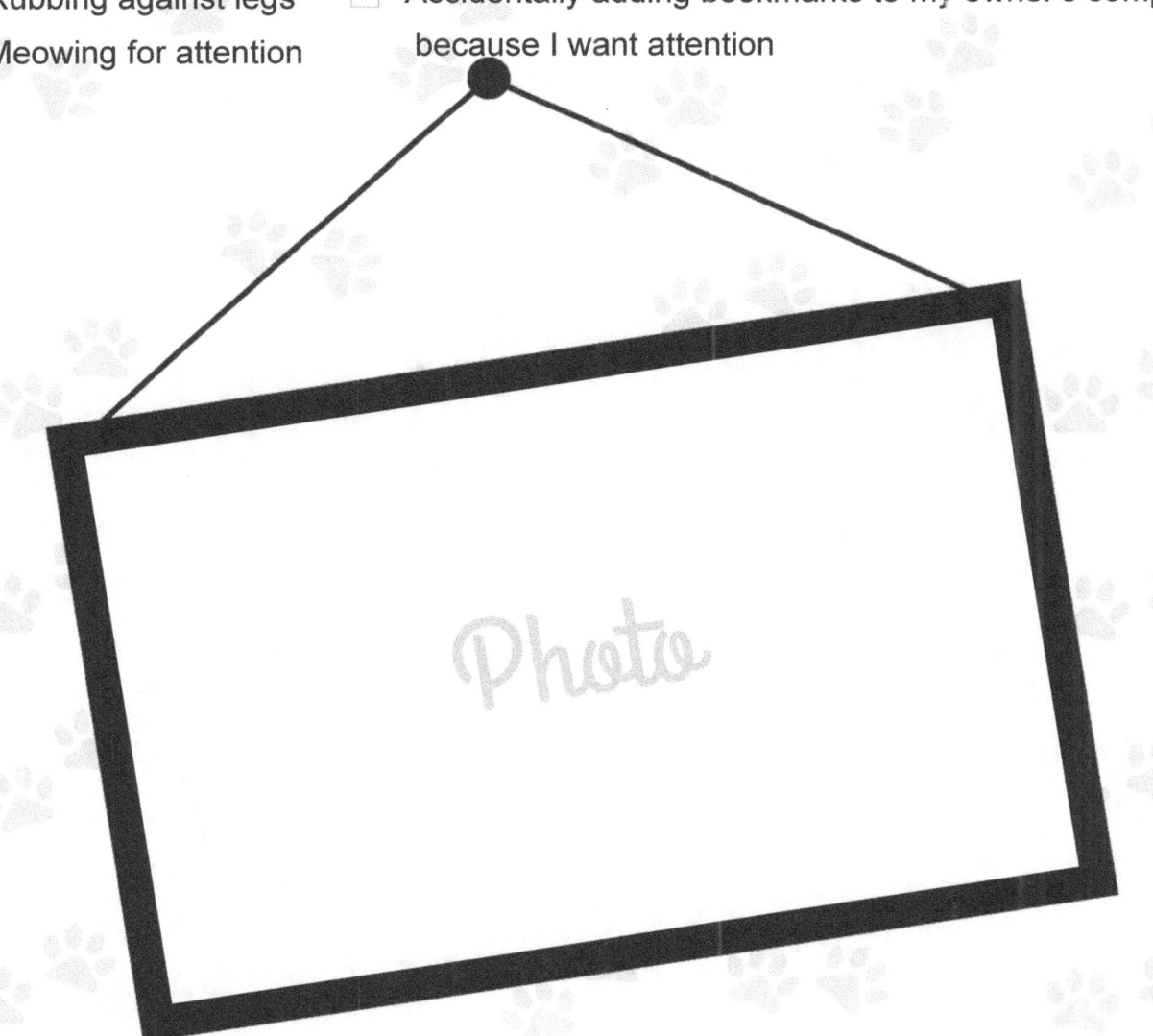

My Favorite Meow-Worker

Dear Meow-Worker, thanks for being my supportive four-legged "co-worker" at home today and I wanted to tell you that I love…

[ ]

This is what it's like "working together" with you at home…

[ ]

This is what I imagine you doing in the other room right now…

[ ]

Today, you make me happy by…

[ ]

Your favorite snack is…	Favorite place to sit is…	Your rating in the Snuggles department is… ☆☆☆☆☆
I am feeding you your favorite…	The times you made me laugh so hard are…	I love it when you…
I could use some more…	I could use a little less…	When you roll over, you…
On our "break time" from work, you love to…		Fave place to frantically run…
When I wash you, you…	My "support system" includes…	I find it funny when…
Some lessons I learned from knowing you are…		Favorite place to leave hairballs is….
Your favorite place to be scratched is….	The sound you make is…	Your favorite place to nap is…
You licked me this many times…	We snuggled this many times…	Favorite TV show is…
You were productive at "work" today by…	Your favorite toy to play with is…	You love to torture the…

Things I love

- [ ] Toys
- [ ] Cat nip
- [ ] Getting snuggles
- [ ] Purring
- [ ] Playtime
- [ ] Headbutting
- [ ] Laser pointers
- [ ] Treats for being cute
- [ ] Rubbing against legs
- [ ] Meowing for attention
- [ ] Sitting on the keyboard
- [ ] Licking my owner's neck
- [ ] "Meetings" with my new manager at home
- [ ] Waking my owner up
- [ ] Receiving the max amount of petting I can get
- [ ] Personal lap warmer
- [ ] Gossiping with my meow-worker
- [ ] Trying to drink my owner's coffee while sitting on the laptop
- [ ] Accidentally adding bookmarks to my owner's computer because I want attention

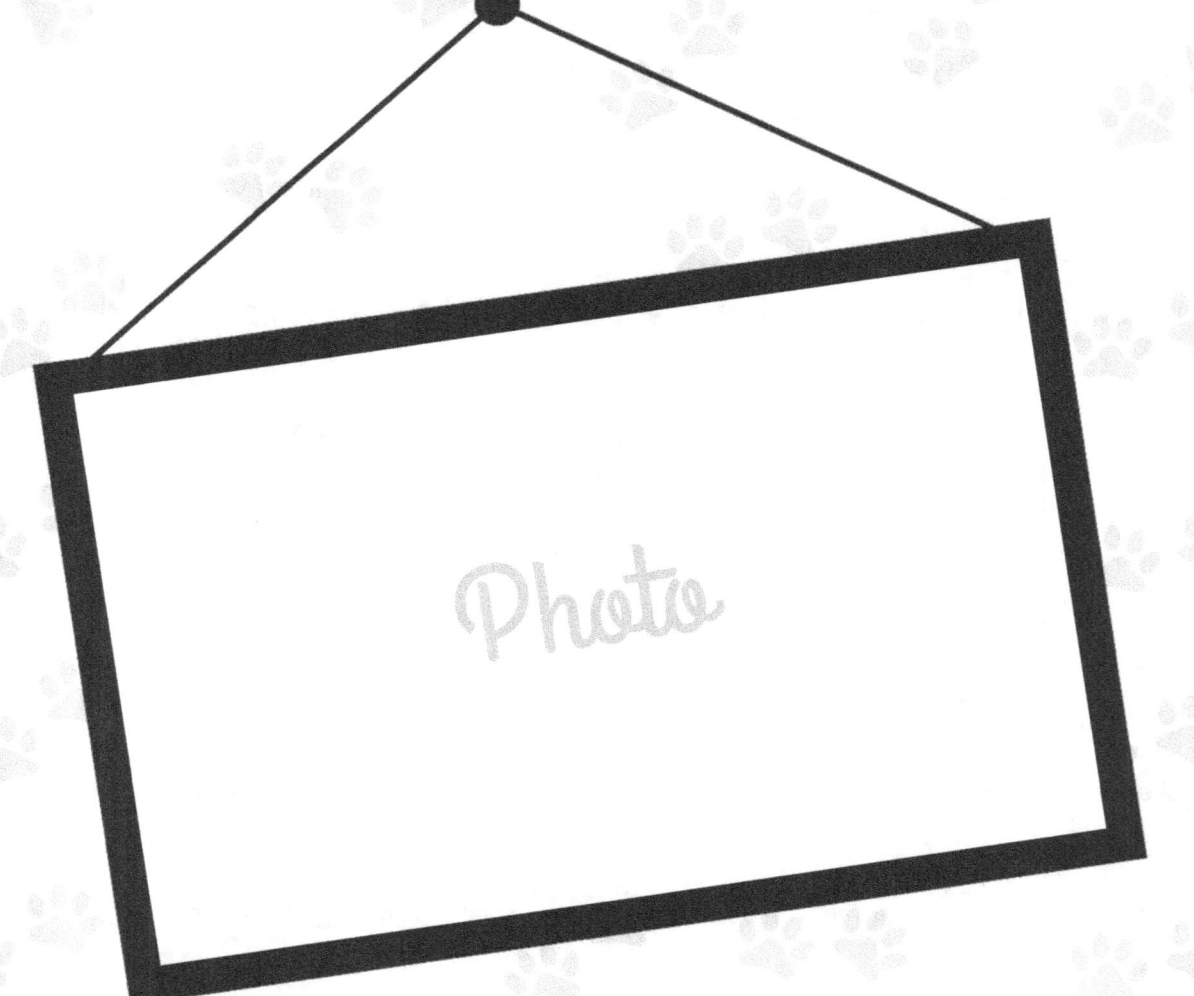

My Favorite Meow-Worker

Dear Meow-Worker, thanks for being my supportive four-legged "co-worker" at home today and I wanted to tell you that I love…

This is what it's like "working together" with you at home…

This is what I imagine you doing in the other room right now…

Today, you make me happy by…

Your favorite snack is… | Favorite place to sit is… | Your rating in the Snuggles department is… ☆☆☆☆☆

I am feeding you your favorite… | The times you made me laugh so hard are… | I love it when you…

I could use some more… | I could use a little less… | When you roll over, you…

On our "break time" from work, you love to… | | Fave place to frantically run..

When I wash you, you… | My "support system" includes… | I find it funny when…

Some lessons I learned from knowing you are… | | Favorite place to leave hairballs is

Your favorite place to be scratched is…. | The sound you make is… | Your favorite place to nap is..

You licked me this many times… | We snuggled this many times… | Favorite TV show is…

You were productive at "work" today by… | Your favorite toy to play with is… | You love to torture the…

Things I love

- [ ] Toys
- [ ] Cat nip
- [ ] Getting snuggles
- [ ] Purring
- [ ] Playtime
- [ ] Headbutting
- [ ] Laser pointers
- [ ] Treats for being cute
- [ ] Rubbing against legs
- [ ] Meowing for attention
- [ ] Sitting on the keyboard
- [ ] Licking my owner's neck
- [ ] "Meetings" with my new manager at home
- [ ] Waking my owner up
- [ ] Receiving the max amount of petting I can get
- [ ] Personal lap warmer
- [ ] Gossiping with my meow-worker
- [ ] Trying to drink my owner's coffee while sitting on the laptop
- [ ] Accidentally adding bookmarks to my owner's computer because I want attention

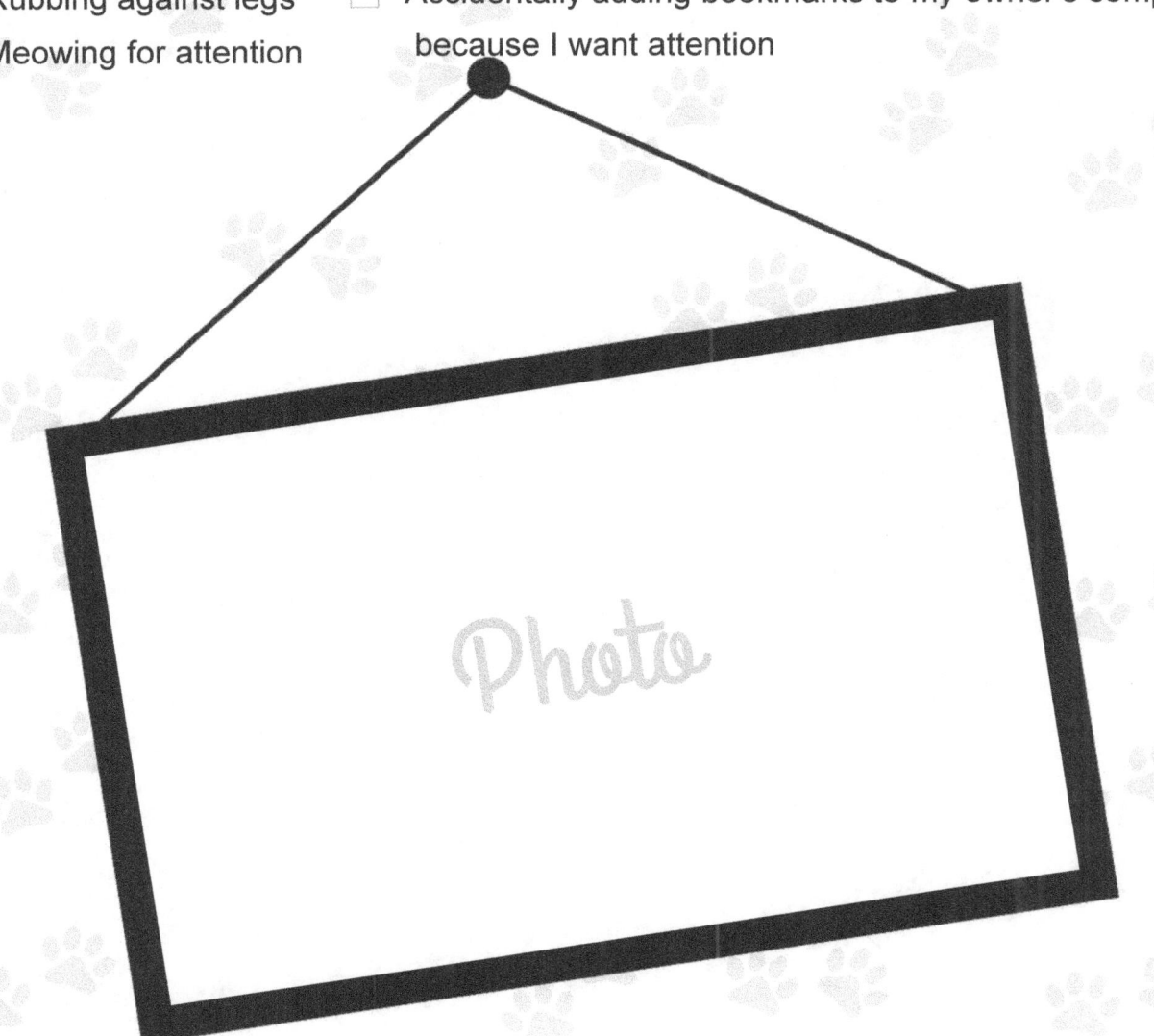

My Favorite Meow-Worker

Dear Meow-Worker, thanks for being my supportive four-legged "co-worker" at home today and I wanted to tell you that I love…

_____

This is what it's like "working together" with you at home…

_____

This is what I imagine you doing in the other room right now…

_____

Today, you make me happy by…

_____

Your favorite snack is…	Favorite place to sit is…	Your rating in the Snuggles department is… ☆☆☆☆☆
I am feeding you your favorite…	The times you made me laugh so hard are…	I love it when you…
I could use some more…	I could use a little less…	When you roll over, you…
On our "break time" from work, you love to…		Fave place to frantically run…
When I wash you, you…	My "support system" includes…	I find it funny when…
Some lessons I learned from knowing you are…		Favorite place to leave hairballs is….
Your favorite place to be scratched is….	The sound you make is…	Your favorite place to nap is…
You licked me this many times…	We snuggled this many times…	Favorite TV show is…
You were productive at "work" today by…	Your favorite toy to play with is…	You love to torture the…

Things I love

- [ ] Toys
- [ ] Cat nip
- [ ] Getting snuggles
- [ ] Purring
- [ ] Playtime
- [ ] Headbutting
- [ ] Laser pointers
- [ ] Treats for being cute
- [ ] Rubbing against legs
- [ ] Meowing for attention
- [ ] Sitting on the keyboard
- [ ] Licking my owner's neck
- [ ] "Meetings" with my new manager at home
- [ ] Waking my owner up
- [ ] Receiving the max amount of petting I can get
- [ ] Personal lap warmer
- [ ] Gossiping with my meow-worker
- [ ] Trying to drink my owner's coffee while sitting on the lap
- [ ] Accidentally adding bookmarks to my owner's computer because I want attention

My Favorite Meow-Worker

Dear Meow-Worker, thanks for being my supportive four-legged "co-worker" at home today and I wanted to tell you that I love…

[ ]

This is what it's like "working together" with you at home…

[ ]

This is what I imagine you doing in the other room right now…

[ ]

Today, you make me happy by…

[ ]

Your favorite snack is…

[ ]

Favorite place to sit is…

[ ]

Your rating in the Snuggles department is… ☆☆☆☆☆

I am feeding you your favorite…

[ ]

The times you made me laugh so hard are…

[ ]

I love it when you…

[ ]

I could use some more…

[ ]

I could use a little less…

[ ]

When you roll over, you…

[ ]

On our "break time" from work, you love to…

[ ]

Fave place to frantically run…

[ ]

When I wash you, you…

[ ]

My "support system" includes…

[ ]

I find it funny when…

[ ]

Some lessons I learned from knowing you are…

[ ]

Favorite place to leave hairballs is…

[ ]

Your favorite place to be scratched is….

[ ]

The sound you make is…

[ ]

Your favorite place to nap is…

[ ]

You licked me this many times…

[ ]

We snuggled this many times…

[ ]

Favorite TV show is…

[ ]

You were productive at "work" today by…

[ ]

Your favorite toy to play with is…

[ ]

You love to torture the…

[ ]

Things I love

- ☐ Toys
- ☐ Cat nip
- ☐ Getting snuggles
- ☐ Purring
- ☐ Playtime
- ☐ Headbutting
- ☐ Laser pointers
- ☐ Treats for being cute
- ☐ Rubbing against legs
- ☐ Meowing for attention
- ☐ Sitting on the keyboard
- ☐ Licking my owner's neck
- ☐ "Meetings" with my new manager at home
- ☐ Waking my owner up
- ☐ Receiving the max amount of petting I can get
- ☐ Personal lap warmer
- ☐ Gossiping with my meow-worker
- ☐ Trying to drink my owner's coffee while sitting on the laptop
- ☐ Accidentally adding bookmarks to my owner's computer because I want attention

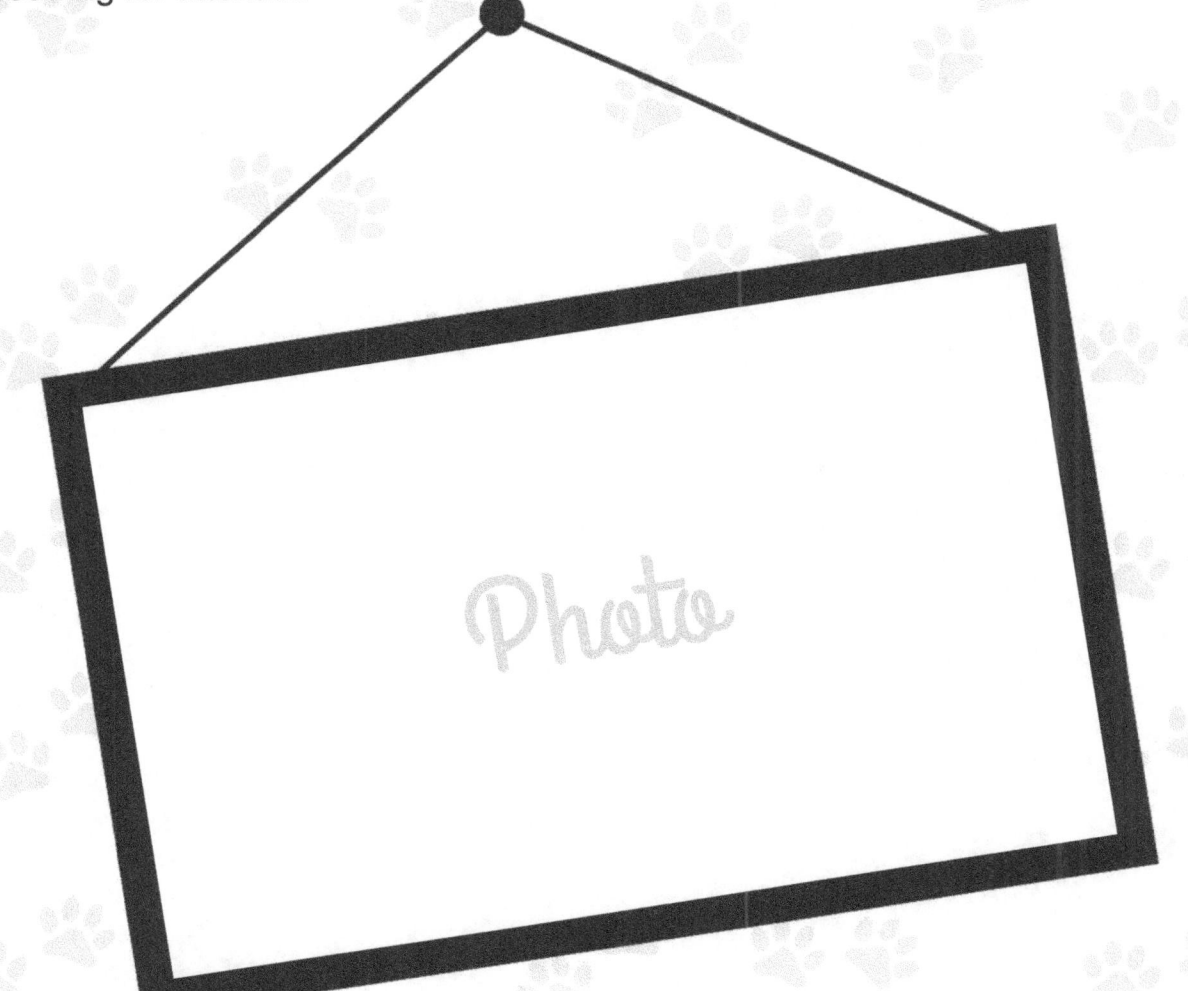

My Favorite Meow-Worker

Dear Meow-Worker, thanks for being my supportive four-legged "co-worker" at home today and I wanted to tell you that I love…

[ ]

This is what it's like "working together" with you at home…

[ ]

This is what I imagine you doing in the other room right now…

[ ]

Today, you make me happy by…

[ ]

Your favorite snack is…
[ ]

Favorite place to sit is…
[ ]

Your rating in the Snuggles department is…
☆ ☆ ☆ ☆ ☆

I am feeding you your favorite…
[ ]

The times you made me laugh so hard are…
[ ]

I love it when you…
[ ]

I could use some more…
[ ]

I could use a little less…
[ ]

When you roll over, you…
[ ]

On our "break time" from work, you love to…
[ ]

Fave place to frantically run…
[ ]

When I wash you, you…
[ ]

My "support system" includes…
[ ]

I find it funny when…
[ ]

Some lessons I learned from knowing you are…
[ ]

Favorite place to leave hairballs is….
[ ]

Your favorite place to be scratched is….
[ ]

The sound you make is…
[ ]

Your favorite place to nap is…
[ ]

You licked me this many times…
[ ]

We snuggled this many times…
[ ]

Favorite TV show is…
[ ]

You were productive at "work" today by…
[ ]

Your favorite toy to play with is…
[ ]

You love to torture the…
[ ]

Things I love

- ☐ Toys
- ☐ Cat nip
- ☐ Getting snuggles
- ☐ Purring
- ☐ Playtime
- ☐ Headbutting
- ☐ Laser pointers
- ☐ Treats for being cute
- ☐ Rubbing against legs
- ☐ Meowing for attention
- ☐ Sitting on the keyboard
- ☐ Licking my owner's neck
- ☐ "Meetings" with my new manager at home
- ☐ Waking my owner up
- ☐ Receiving the max amount of petting I can get
- ☐ Personal lap warmer
- ☐ Gossiping with my meow-worker
- ☐ Trying to drink my owner's coffee while sitting on the lapt
- ☐ Accidentally adding bookmarks to my owner's computer because I want attention

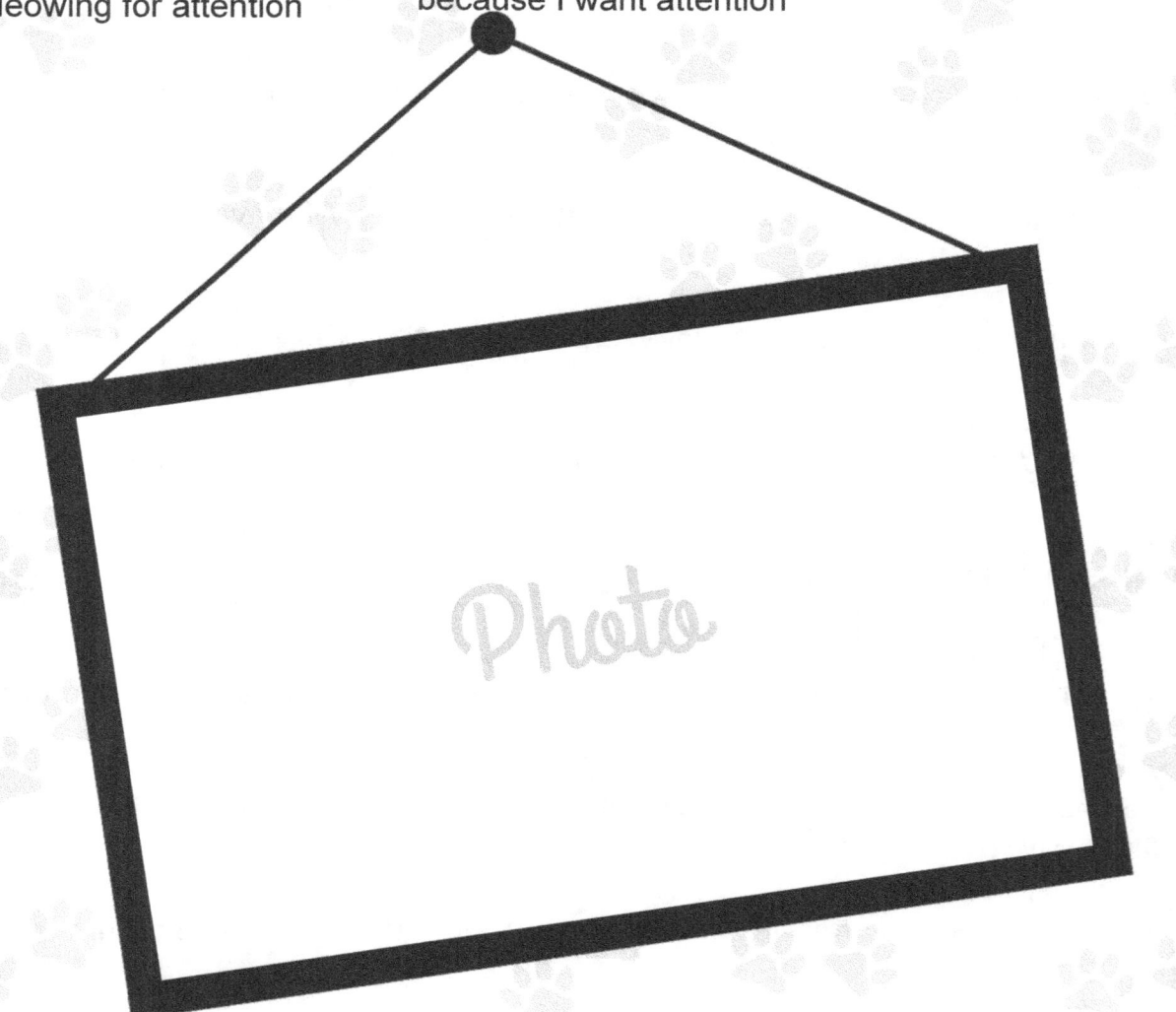

My Favorite Meow-Worker

Dear Meow-Worker, thanks for being my supportive four-legged "co-worker" at home today and I wanted to tell you that I love…

[ ]

This is what it's like "working together" with you at home…

[ ]

This is what I imagine you doing in the other room right now…

[ ]

Today, you make me happy by…

[ ]

Your favorite snack is… | Favorite place to sit is… | Your rating in the Snuggles department is… ☆☆☆☆☆

[ ] | [ ] |

I am feeding you your favorite… | The times you made me laugh so hard are… | I love it when you…

[ ] | [ ] | [ ]

I could use some more… | I could use a little less… | When you roll over, you…

[ ] | [ ] | [ ]

On our "break time" from work, you love to… | | Fave place to frantically run…

[ ] | | [ ]

When I wash you, you… | My "support system" includes… | I find it funny when…

[ ] | [ ] | [ ]

Some lessons I learned from knowing you are… | | Favorite place to leave hairballs is

[ ] | | [ ]

Your favorite place to be scratched is… | The sound you make is… | Your favorite place to nap is.

[ ] | [ ] | [ ]

You licked me this many times… | We snuggled this many times… | Favorite TV show is…

[ ] | [ ] | [ ]

You were productive at "work" today by… | Your favorite toy to play with is… | You love to torture the…

[ ] | [ ] | [ ]

Things I love

- [ ] Toys
- [ ] Cat nip
- [ ] Getting snuggles
- [ ] Purring
- [ ] Playtime
- [ ] Headbutting
- [ ] Laser pointers
- [ ] Treats for being cute
- [ ] Rubbing against legs
- [ ] Meowing for attention
- [ ] Sitting on the keyboard
- [ ] Licking my owner's neck
- [ ] "Meetings" with my new manager at home
- [ ] Waking my owner up
- [ ] Receiving the max amount of petting I can get
- [ ] Personal lap warmer
- [ ] Gossiping with my meow-worker
- [ ] Trying to drink my owner's coffee while sitting on the laptop
- [ ] Accidentally adding bookmarks to my owner's computer because I want attention

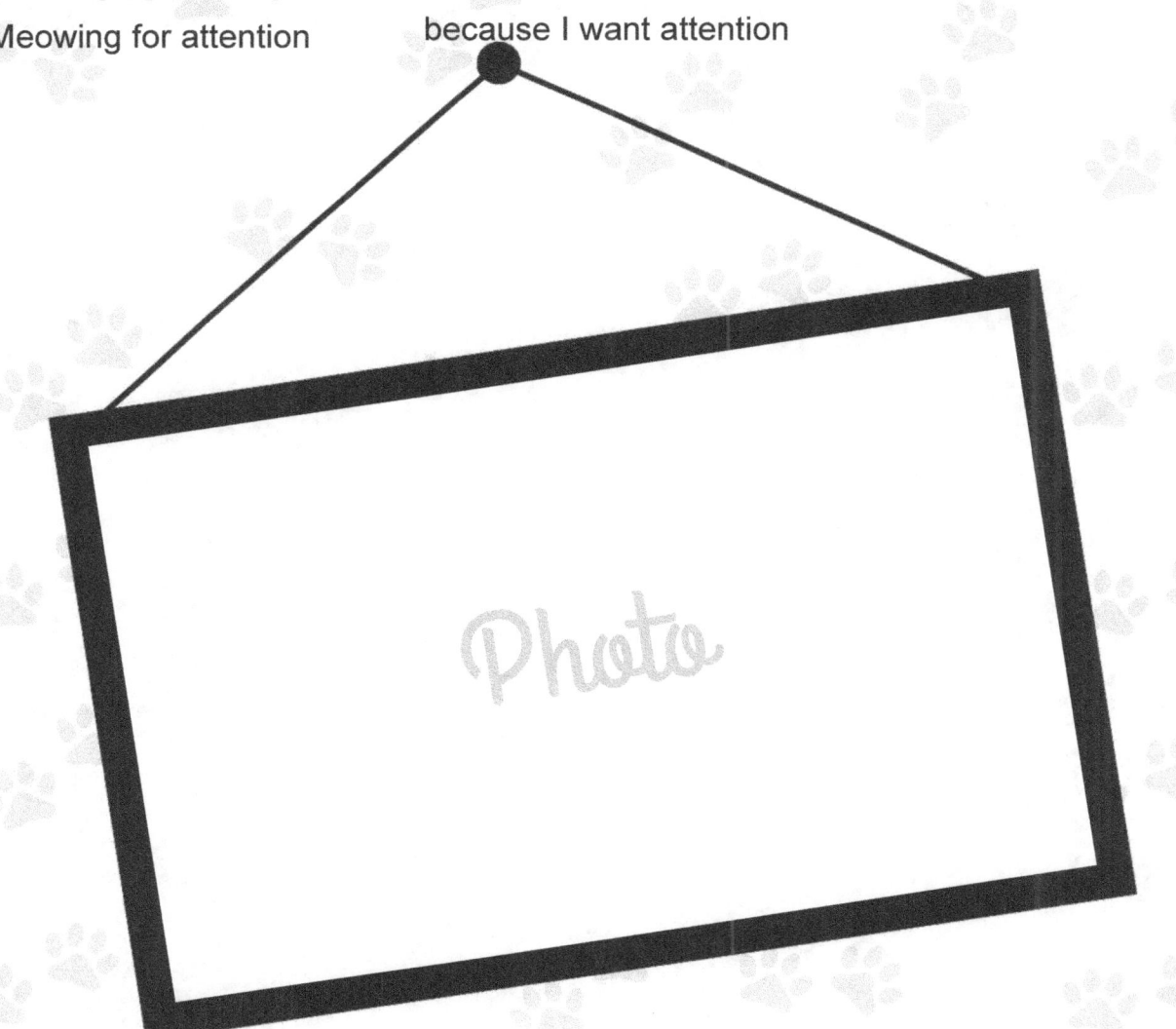

My Favorite Meow-Worker

Dear Meow-Worker, thanks for being my supportive four-legged "co-worker" at home today and I wanted to tell you that I love…

This is what it's like "working together" with you at home…

This is what I imagine you doing in the other room right now…

Today, you make me happy by…

Your favorite snack is… | Favorite place to sit is… | Your rating in the Snuggles department is… ☆☆☆☆☆

I am feeding you your favorite… | The times you made me laugh so hard are… | I love it when you…

I could use some more… | I could use a little less… | When you roll over, you…

On our "break time" from work, you love to… | Fave place to frantically run…

When I wash you, you… | My "support system" includes… | I find it funny when…

Some lessons I learned from knowing you are… | Favorite place to leave hairballs is….

Your favorite place to be scratched is….The sound you make is… | Your favorite place to nap is…

You licked me this many times… | We snuggled this many times… | Favorite TV show is…

You were productive at "work" today by…Your favorite toy to play with is… | You love to torture the…

Things I love

- [ ] Toys
- [ ] Cat nip
- [ ] Getting snuggles
- [ ] Purring
- [ ] Playtime
- [ ] Headbutting
- [ ] Laser pointers
- [ ] Treats for being cute
- [ ] Rubbing against legs
- [ ] Meowing for attention
- [ ] Sitting on the keyboard
- [ ] Licking my owner's neck
- [ ] "Meetings" with my new manager at home
- [ ] Waking my owner up
- [ ] Receiving the max amount of petting I can get
- [ ] Personal lap warmer
- [ ] Gossiping with my meow-worker
- [ ] Trying to drink my owner's coffee while sitting on the lap
- [ ] Accidentally adding bookmarks to my owner's computer because I want attention

Photo

My Favorite Meow-Worker

Dear Meow-Worker, thanks for being my supportive four-legged "co-worker" at home today and I wanted to tell you that I love…

[   ]

This is what it's like "working together" with you at home…

[   ]

This is what I imagine you doing in the other room right now…

[   ]

Today, you make me happy by…

[   ]

Your favorite snack is…	Favorite place to sit is…	Your rating in the Snuggles department is… ☆☆☆☆☆
[ ]	[ ]	
I am feeding you your favorite…	The times you made me laugh so hard are…	I love it when you…
[ ]	[ ]	[ ]
I could use some more…	I could use a little less…	When you roll over, you…
[ ]	[ ]	[ ]
On our "break time" from work, you love to…		Fave place to frantically run…
[ ]		[ ]
When I wash you, you…	My "support system" includes…	I find it funny when…
[ ]	[ ]	[ ]
Some lessons I learned from knowing you are…		Favorite place to leave hairballs is
[ ]		[ ]
Your favorite place to be scratched is…	The sound you make is…	Your favorite place to nap is…
[ ]	[ ]	[ ]
You licked me this many times…	We snuggled this many times…	Favorite TV show is…
[ ]	[ ]	[ ]
You were productive at "work" today by…	Your favorite toy to play with is…	You love to torture the…
[ ]	[ ]	[ ]

Things I love

- ☑ Toys
- ☐ Cat nip
- ☐ Getting snuggles
- ☐ Purring
- ☐ Playtime
- ☐ Headbutting
- ☐ Laser pointers
- ☐ Treats for being cute
- ☐ Rubbing against legs
- ☐ Meowing for attention
- ☐ Sitting on the keyboard
- ☐ Licking my owner's neck
- ☐ "Meetings" with my new manager at home
- ☐ Waking my owner up
- ☑ Receiving the max amount of petting I can get
- ☐ Personal lap warmer
- ☐ Gossiping with my meow-worker
- ☐ Trying to drink my owner's coffee while sitting on the laptop
- ☐ Accidentally adding bookmarks to my owner's computer because I want attention

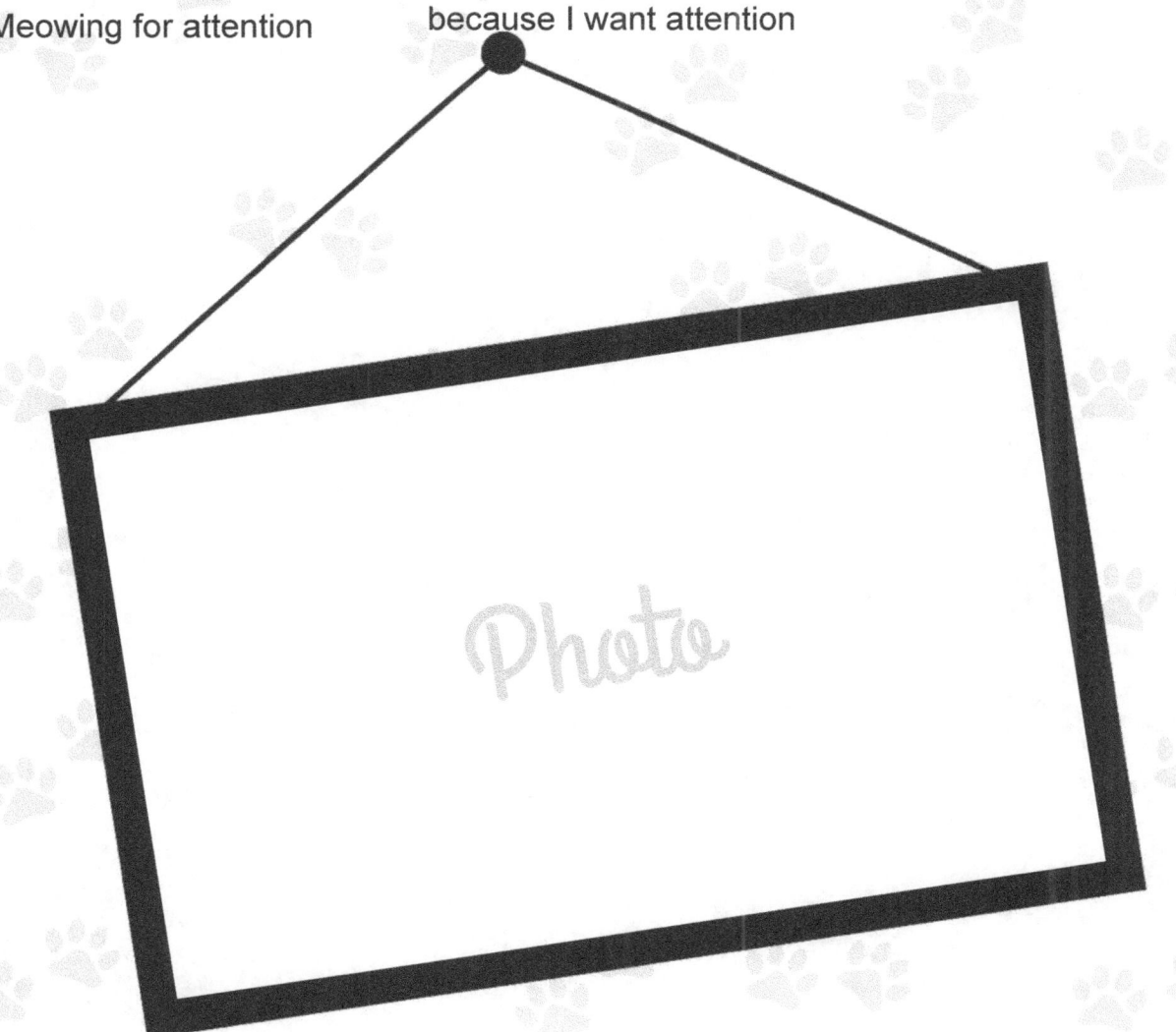

My Favorite Meow-Worker

Dear Meow-Worker, thanks for being my supportive four-legged "co-worker" at home today and I wanted to tell you that I love…

_____

This is what it's like "working together" with you at home…

_____

This is what I imagine you doing in the other room right now…

_____

Today, you make me happy by…

_____

Your favorite snack is…	Favorite place to sit is…	Your rating in the Snuggles department's… ☆☆☆☆☆
I am feeding you your favorite…	The times you made me laugh so hard are…	I love t when you…
I could use some more…	I could use a little less…	When you roll over, you…
On our "break time" from work, you love to…		Fave place to frantically run…
When I wash you, you…	My "support system" includes…	I find it funny when…
Some lessons I learned from knowing you are…		Favorite place to leave hairballs is….
Your favorite place to be scratched is….	The sound you make is…	Your favorite place to nap is…
You licked me this many times…	We snuggled this many times…	Favorite TV show is…
You were productive at "work" today by…	Your favorite toy to play with is…	You love to torture the…

Things I love

- ☐ Toys
- ☐ Cat nip
- ☐ Getting snuggles
- ☐ Purring
- ☐ Playtime
- ☐ Headbutting
- ☐ Laser pointers
- ☐ Treats for being cute
- ☐ Rubbing against legs
- ☐ Meowing for attention
- ☐ Sitting on the keyboard
- ☐ Licking my owner's neck
- ☐ "Meetings" with my new manager at home
- ☐ Waking my owner up
- ☐ Receiving the max amount of petting I can get
- ☐ Personal lap warmer
- ☐ Gossiping with my meow-worker
- ☐ Trying to drink my owner's coffee while sitting on the lapt
- ☐ Accidentally adding bookmarks to my owner's computer because I want attention

My Favorite Meow-Worker

Dear Meow-Worker, thanks for being my supportive four-legged "co-worker" at home today and I wanted to tell you that I love…

This is what it's like "working together" with you at home…

This is what I imagine you doing in the other room right now…

Today, you make me happy by…

Your favorite snack is…   Favorite place to sit is…   Your rating in the Snuggles department is… ☆☆☆☆☆

I am feeding you your favorite…   The times you made me laugh so hard are…   I love it when you…

I could use some more…   I could use a little less…   When you roll over, you…

On our "break time" from work, you love to…   Fave place to frantically run.

When I wash you, you…   My "support system" includes…   I find it funny when…

Some lessons I learned from knowing you are…   Favorite place to leave hairballs is

Your favorite place to be scratched is….   The sound you make is…   Your favorite place to nap is.

You licked me this many times…   We snuggled this many times…   Favorite TV show is…

You were productive at "work" today by…   Your favorite toy to play with is…   You love to torture the…

Things I love

- ☐ Toys
- ☐ Cat nip
- ☐ Getting snuggles
- ☐ Purring
- ☐ Playtime
- ☐ Headbutting
- ☐ Laser pointers
- ☐ Treats for being cute
- ☐ Rubbing against legs
- ☐ Meowing for attention
- ☐ Sitting on the keyboard
- ☐ Licking my owner's neck
- ☐ "Meetings" with my new manager at home
- ☐ Waking my owner up
- ☐ Receiving the max amount of petting I can get
- ☐ Personal lap warmer
- ☐ Gossiping with my meow-worker
- ☐ Trying to drink my owner's coffee while sitting on the laptop
- ☐ Accidentally adding bookmarks to my owner's computer because I want attention

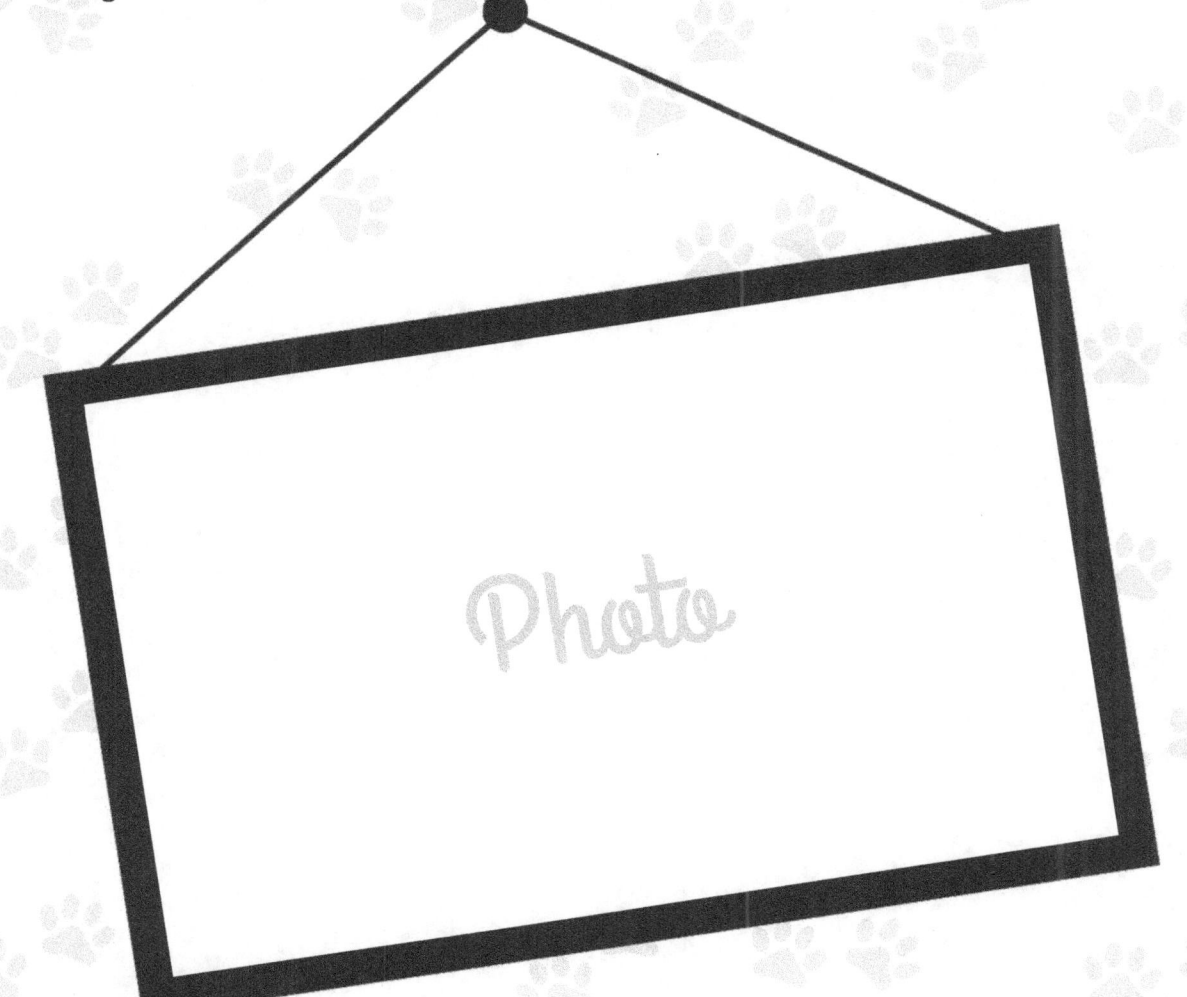

My Favorite Meow-Worker

Dear Meow-Worker, thanks for being my supportive four-legged "co-worker" at home today and I wanted to tell you that I love…

This is what it's like "working together" with you at home…

This is what I imagine you doing in the other room right now…

Today, you make me happy by…

Your favorite snack is…

Favorite place to sit is…

Your rating in the Snuggles department is… ☆☆☆☆☆

I am feeding you your favorite…

The times you made me laugh so hard are…

I love it when you…

I could use some more…

I could use a little less…

When you roll over, you…

On our "break time" from work, you love to…

Fave place to frantically run…

When I wash you, you…

My "support system" includes…

I find it funny when…

Some lessons I learned from knowing you are…

Favorite place to leave hairballs is….

Your favorite place to be scratched is….

The sound you make is…

Your favorite place to nap is…

You licked me this many times…

We snuggled this many times…

Favorite TV show is…

You were productive at "work" today by…

Your favorite toy to play with is…

You love to torture the…

Things I love

- ☐ Toys
- ☐ Cat nip
- ☐ Getting snuggles
- ☐ Purring
- ☐ Playtime
- ☐ Headbutting
- ☐ Laser pointers
- ☐ Treats for being cute
- ☐ Rubbing against legs
- ☐ Meowing for attention
- ☐ Sitting on the keyboard
- ☐ Licking my owner's neck
- ☐ "Meetings" with my new manager at home
- ☐ Waking my owner up
- ☐ Receiving the max amount of petting I can get
- ☐ Personal lap warmer
- ☐ Gossiping with my meow-worker
- ☐ Trying to drink my owner's coffee while sitting on the lap
- ☐ Accidentally adding bookmarks to my owner's computer because I want attention

Photo

My Favorite Meow-Worker

Dear Meow-Worker, thanks for being my supportive four-legged "co-worker" at home today and I wanted to tell you that I love…

[   ]

This is what it's like "working together" with you at home…

[   ]

This is what I imagine you doing in the other room right now…

[   ]

Today, you make me happy by…

[   ]

Your favorite snack is…	Favorite place to sit is…	Your rating in the Snuggles department is… ☆☆☆☆☆
[ ]	[ ]	
I am feeding you your favorite…	The times you made me laugh so hard are…	I love it when you…
[ ]	[ ]	[ ]
I could use some more…	I could use a little less…	When you roll over, you…
[ ]	[ ]	[ ]
On our "break time" from work, you love to…		Fave place to frantically run..
[ ]		[ ]
When I wash you, you…	My "support system" includes…	I find it funny when…
[ ]	[ ]	[ ]
Some lessons I learned from knowing you are…		Favorite place to leave hairballs is
[ ]		[ ]
Your favorite place to be scratched is….	The sound you make is…	Your favorite place to nap is..
[ ]	[ ]	[ ]
You licked me this many times…	We snuggled this many times…	Favorite TV show is…
[ ]	[ ]	[ ]
You were productive at "work" today by…	Your favorite toy to play with is…	You love to torture the…
[ ]	[ ]	[ ]

Things I love

- ☑ Toys
- ☐ Cat nip
- ☐ Getting snuggles
- ☐ Purring
- ☐ Playtime
- ☐ Headbutting
- ☐ Laser pointers
- ☐ Treats for being cute
- ☐ Rubbing against legs
- ☐ Meowing for attention
- ☐ Sitting on the keyboard
- ☐ Licking my owner's neck
- ☐ "Meetings" with my new manager at home
- ☐ Waking my owner up
- ☐ Receiving the max amount of petting I can get
- ☐ Personal lap warmer
- ☐ Gossiping with my meow-worker
- ☐ Trying to drink my owner's coffee while sitting on the laptop
- ☐ Accidentally adding bookmarks to my owner's computer because I want attention

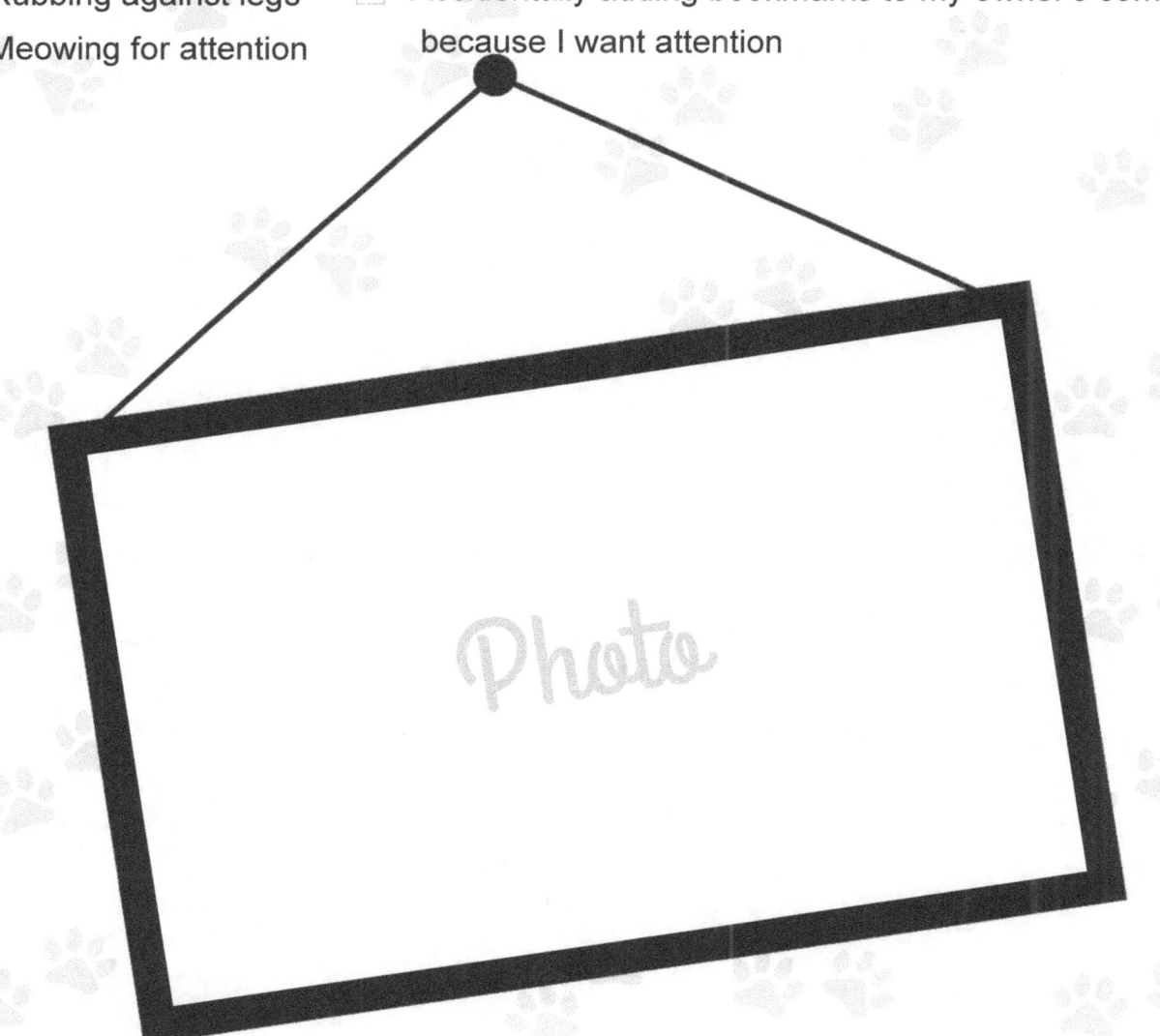

My Favorite Meow-Worker

Dear Meow-Worker, thanks for being my supportive four-legged "co-worker" at home today and I wanted to tell you that I love…

This is what it's like "working together" with you at home…

This is what I imagine you doing in the other room right now…

Today, you make me happy by…

Your favorite snack is…　　Favorite place to sit is…　　Your rating in the Snuggles department is… ☆☆☆☆☆

I am feeding you your favorite…　　The times you made me laugh so hard are…　　I love it when you…

I could use some more…　　I could use a little less…　　When you roll over, you…

On our "break time" from work, you love to…　　Fave place to frantically run…

When I wash you, you…　　My "support system" includes…　　I find it funny when…

Some lessons I learned from knowing you are…　　Favorite place to leave hairballs is….

Your favorite place to be scratched is….　　The sound you make is…　　Your favorite place to nap is…

You licked me this many times…　　We snuggled this many times…　　Favorite TV show is…

You were productive at "work" today by…　　Your favorite toy to play with is…　　You love to torture the…

Things I love

- ☐ Toys
- ☐ Cat nip
- ☐ Getting snuggles
- ☐ Purring
- ☐ Playtime
- ☐ Headbutting
- ☐ Laser pointers
- ☐ Treats for being cute
- ☐ Rubbing against legs
- ☐ Meowing for attention
- ☐ Sitting on the keyboard
- ☐ Licking my owner's neck
- ☐ "Meetings" with my new manager at home
- ☐ Waking my owner up
- ☐ Receiving the max amount of petting I can get
- ☐ Personal lap warmer
- ☐ Gossiping with my meow-worker
- ☐ Trying to drink my owner's coffee while sitting on the laptop
- ☐ Accidentally adding bookmarks to my owner's computer because I want attention

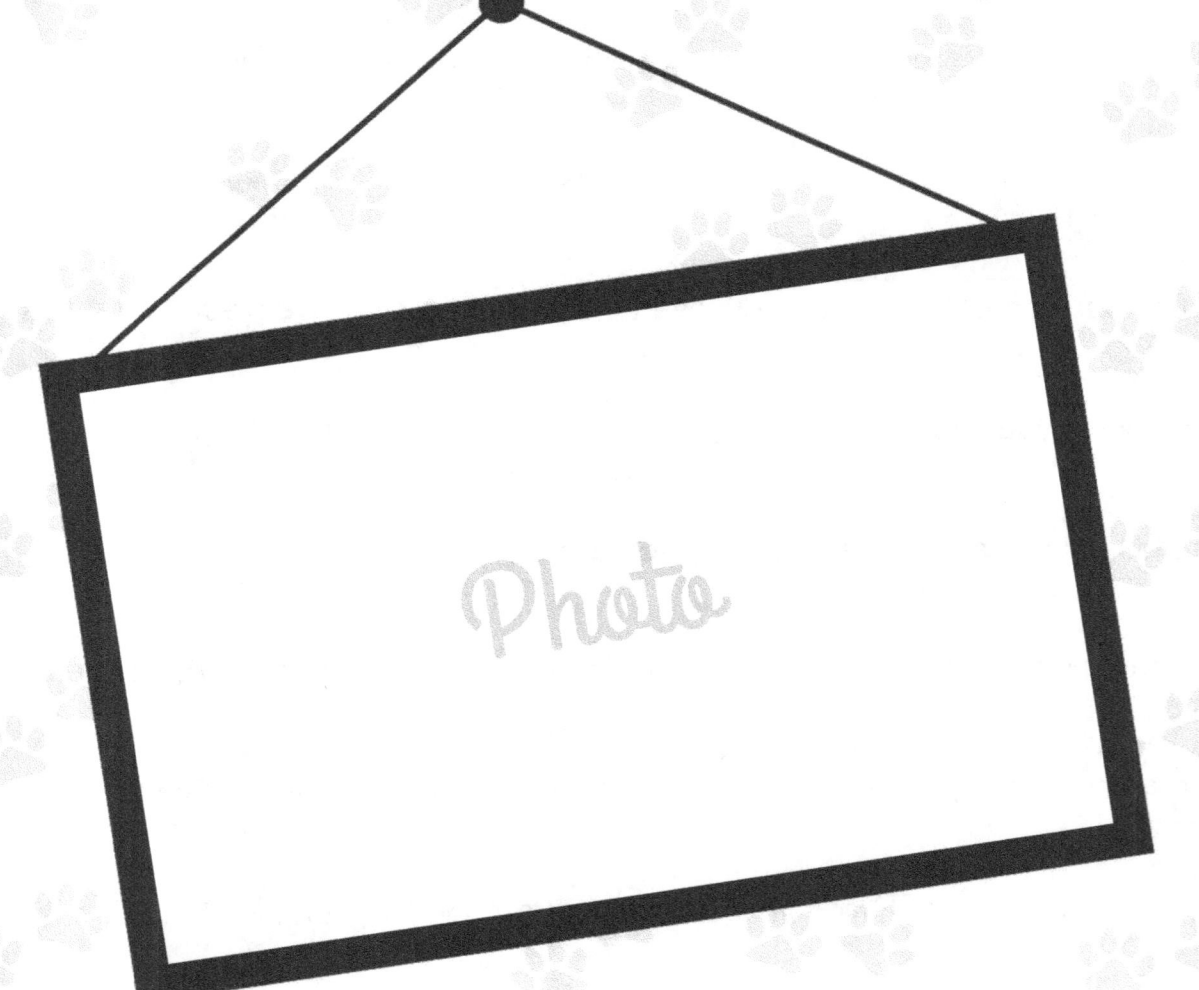

My Favorite Meow-Worker

Dear Meow-Worker, thanks for being my supportive four-legged "co-worker" at home today and I wanted to tell you that I love…

This is what it's like "working together" with you at home…

This is what I imagine you doing in the other room right now…

Today, you make me happy by…

Your favorite snack is… Favorite place to sit is… Your rating in the Snuggles department is… ☆☆☆☆☆

I am feeding you your favorite… The times you made me laugh so hard are… I love it when you…

I could use some more… I could use a little less… When you roll over, you…

On our "break time" from work, you love to… Fave place to frantically run…

When I wash you, you… My "support system" includes… I find it funny when…

Some lessons I learned from knowing you are… Favorite place to leave hairballs is…

Your favorite place to be scratched is… The sound you make is… Your favorite place to nap is.

You licked me this many times… We snuggled this many times… Favorite TV show is…

You were productive at "work" today by… Your favorite toy to play with is… You love to torture the…

Things I love

- [ ] Toys
- [ ] Cat nip
- [ ] Getting snuggles
- [ ] Purring
- [ ] Playtime
- [ ] Headbutting
- [ ] Laser pointers
- [ ] Treats for being cute
- [ ] Rubbing against legs
- [ ] Meowing for attention
- [ ] Sitting on the keyboard
- [ ] Licking my owner's neck
- [ ] "Meetings" with my new manager at home
- [ ] Waking my owner up
- [ ] Receiving the max amount of petting I can get
- [ ] Personal lap warmer
- [ ] Gossiping with my meow-worker
- [ ] Trying to drink my owner's coffee while sitting on the laptop
- [ ] Accidentally adding bookmarks to my owner's computer because I want attention

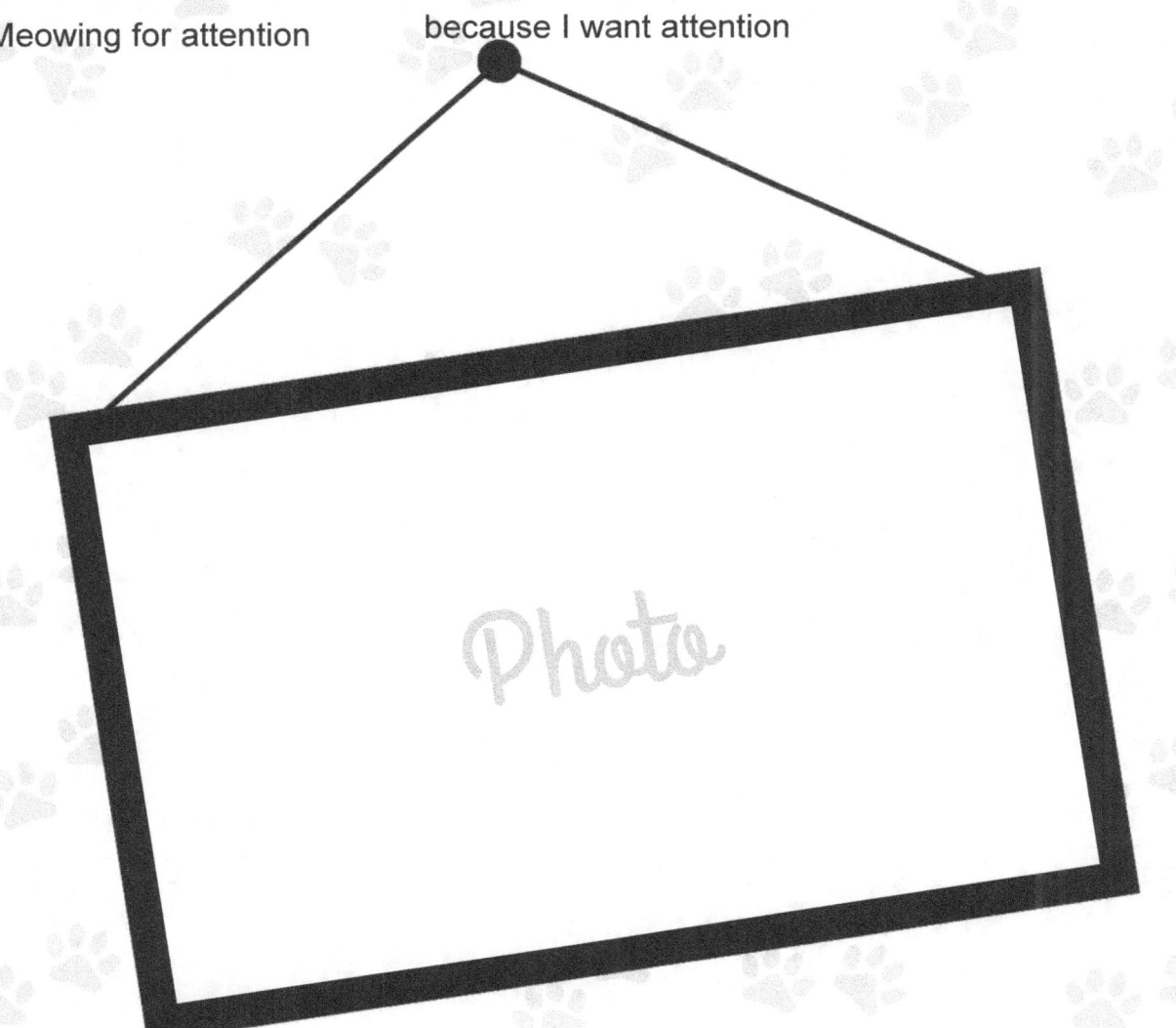

My Favorite Meow-Worker

Dear Meow-Worker, thanks for being my supportive four-legged "co-worker" at home today and I wanted to tell you that I love…

This is what it's like "working together" with you at home…

This is what I imagine you doing in the other room right now…

Today, you make me happy by…

Your favorite snack is… | Favorite place to sit is… | Your rating in the Snuggles department is… ☆☆☆☆☆

I am feeding you your favorite… | The times you made me laugh so hard are… | I love it when you…

I could use some more… | I could use a little less… | When you roll over, you…

On our "break time" from work, you love to… | | Fave place to frantically run…

When I wash you, you… | My "support system" includes… | I find it funny when…

Some lessons I learned from knowing you are… | | Favorite place to leave hairballs is….

Your favorite place to be scratched is…. | The sound you make is… | Your favorite place to nap is…

You licked me this many times… | We snuggled this many times… | Favorite TV show is…

You were productive at "work" today by… | Your favorite toy to play with is… | You love to torture the…

Things I love

- ☐ Toys
- ☐ Cat nip
- ☐ Getting snuggles
- ☐ Purring
- ☐ Playtime
- ☐ Headbutting
- ☐ Laser pointers
- ☐ Treats for being cute
- ☐ Rubbing against legs
- ☐ Meowing for attention
- ☐ Sitting on the keyboard
- ☐ Licking my owner's neck
- ☐ "Meetings" with my new manager at home
- ☐ Waking my owner up
- ☐ Receiving the max amount of petting I can get
- ☐ Personal lap warmer
- ☐ Gossiping with my meow-worker
- ☐ Trying to drink my owner's coffee while sitting on the lap
- ☐ Accidentally adding bookmarks to my owner's computer because I want attention

My Favorite Meow-Worker

Dear Meow-Worker, thanks for being my supportive four-legged "co-worker" at home today and I wanted to tell you that I love…

[ ]

This is what it's like "working together" with you at home…

[ ]

This is what I imagine you doing in the other room right now…

[ ]

Today, you make me happy by…

[ ]

Your favorite snack is...	Favorite place to sit is...	Your rating in the Snuggles department is... ☆☆☆☆☆
I am feeding you your favorite...	The times you made me laugh so hard are...	I love it when you...
I could use some more...	I could use a little less...	When you roll over, you...
On our "break time" from work, you love to...		Fave place to frantically run..
When I wash you, you...	My "support system" includes...	I find it funny when...
Some lessons I learned from knowing you are...		Favorite place to leave hairballs is
Your favorite place to be scratched is….	The sound you make is…	Your favorite place to nap is..
You licked me this many times…	We snuggled this many times…	Favorite TV show is…
You were productive at "work" today by…	Your favorite toy to play with is…	You love to torture the…

Things I love

- ☑ Toys
- ☐ Cat nip
- ☐ Getting snuggles
- ☐ Purring
- ☐ Playtime
- ☐ Headbutting
- ☐ Laser pointers
- ☐ Treats for being cute
- ☐ Rubbing against legs
- ☐ Meowing for attention

- ☐ Sitting on the keyboard
- ☐ Licking my owner's neck
- ☐ "Meetings" with my new manager at home
- ☐ Waking my owner up
- ☐ Receiving the max amount of petting I can get
- ☐ Personal lap warmer
- ☐ Gossiping with my meow-worker
- ☐ Trying to drink my owner's coffee while sitting on the laptop
- ☐ Accidentally adding bookmarks to my owner's computer because I want attention

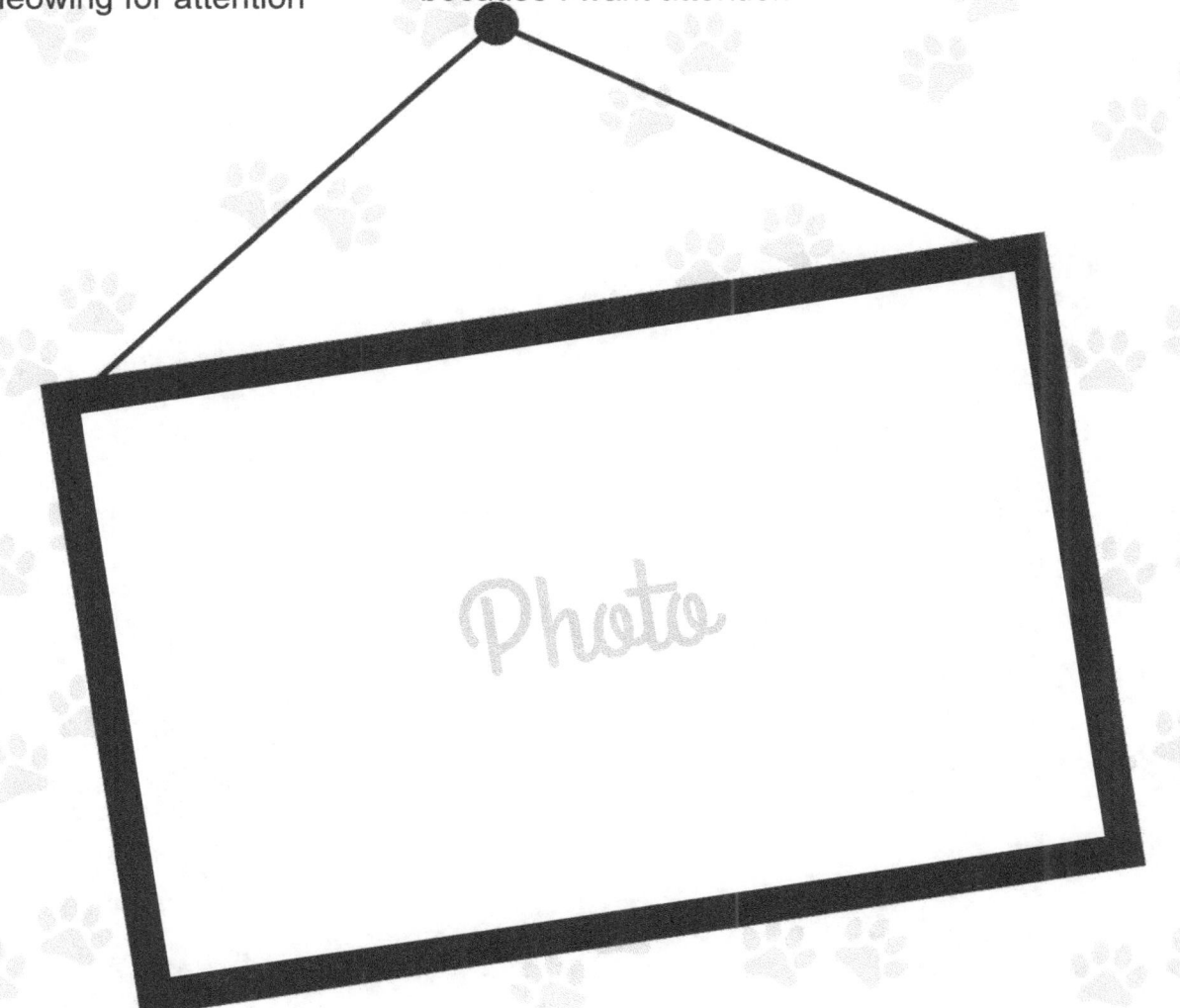

My Favorite Meow-Worker

Dear Meow-Worker, thanks for being my supportive four-legged "co-worker" at home today and I wanted to tell you that I love…

This is what it's like "working together" with you at home…

This is what I imagine you doing in the other room right now…

Today, you make me happy by…

Your favorite snack is… | Favorite place to sit is… | Your rating in the Snuggles department is… ☆☆☆☆☆

I am feeding you your favorite… | The times you made me laugh so hard are… | I love t when you…

I could use some more… | I could use a little less… | When you roll over, you…

On our "break time" from work, you love to… | | Fave place to frantically run…

When I wash you, you… | My "support system" includes… | I find it funny when…

Some lessons I learned from knowing you are… | | Favorite place to leave hairballs is….

Your favorite place to be scratched is…. | The sound you make is… | Your favorite place to nap is…

You licked me this many times… | We snuggled this many times… | Favorite TV show is…

You were productive at "work" today by… | Your favorite toy to play with is… | You love to torture the…

Things I love

- ☐ Toys
- ☐ Cat nip
- ☐ Getting snuggles
- ☐ Purring
- ☐ Playtime
- ☐ Headbutting
- ☐ Laser pointers
- ☐ Treats for being cute
- ☐ Rubbing against legs
- ☐ Meowing for attention

- ☐ Sitting on the keyboard
- ☐ Licking my owner's neck
- ☐ "Meetings" with my new manager at home
- ☐ Waking my owner up
- ☐ Receiving the max amount of petting I can get
- ☐ Personal lap warmer
- ☐ Gossiping with my meow-worker
- ☐ Trying to drink my owner's coffee while sitting on the lapt
- ☐ Accidentally adding bookmarks to my owner's computer because I want attention

Photo

My Favorite Meow-Worker

Dear Meow-Worker, thanks for being my supportive four-legged "co-worker" at home today and I wanted to tell you that I love…

This is what it's like "working together" with you at home…

This is what I imagine you doing in the other room right now…

Today, you make me happy by…

Your favorite snack is…   Favorite place to sit is…   Your rating in the Snuggles department is… ☆☆☆☆☆

I am feeding you your favorite…   The times you made me laugh so hard are…   I love it when you…

I could use some more…   I could use a little less…   When you roll over, you…

On our "break time" from work, you love to…   Fave place to frantically run…

When I wash you, you…   My "support system" includes…   I find it funny when…

Some lessons I learned from knowing you are…   Favorite place to leave hairballs is…

Your favorite place to be scratched is….The sound you make is…   Your favorite place to nap is…

You licked me this many times…   We snuggled this many times…   Favorite TV show is…

You were productive at "work" today by…Your favorite toy to play with is…   You love to torture the…

Things I love

- [ ] Toys
- [ ] Cat nip
- [ ] Getting snuggles
- [ ] Purring
- [ ] Playtime
- [ ] Headbutting
- [ ] Laser pointers
- [ ] Treats for being cute
- [ ] Rubbing against legs
- [ ] Meowing for attention
- [ ] Sitting on the keyboard
- [ ] Licking my owner's neck
- [ ] "Meetings" with my new manager at home
- [ ] Waking my owner up
- [ ] Receiving the max amount of petting I can get
- [ ] Personal lap warmer
- [ ] Gossiping with my meow-worker
- [ ] Trying to drink my owner's coffee while sitting on the laptop
- [ ] Accidentally adding bookmarks to my owner's computer because I want attention

www.ingramcontent.com/pod-product-compliance
Lightning Source LLC
Chambersburg PA
CBHW081232080526
44587CB00022B/3907